EXPLORING
YOUR DREAMS

EXPLORING YOUR DREAMS

How to use dreams for personal growth and creative inspiration

Ruth Snowden

howtobooks

Published by How To Books Ltd
Spring Hill House, Spring Hill Road
Begbroke, Oxford OX5 1RX
Tel: (01865) 375794. Fax: (01865) 379162
info@howtobooks.co.uk
www.howtobooks.co.uk

How To Books greatly reduce the carbon footprint of their books by sourcing their
typesetting and printing in the UK.

British Library Cataloguing in Publication Data
A catalogue record for this book is available from the British Library

ISBN: 978 1 84528 466 4

Cover design by Baseline Arts, Oxford
Produced for How To Books by Deer Park Productions, Tavistock
Typeset by Kestrel Data, Exeter
Printed and bound in Great Britain by MPG Books Group, Bodmin, Cornwall

NOTE: The material contained in this book is set out in good faith for general guidance
and no liability can be accepted for loss or expense incurred as a result of relying in
particular circumstances on statements made in the book. The laws and regulations
are complex and liable to change, and readers should check the current position with
the relevant authorities before making personal arrangements.

Contents

Illustrations and tables

Preface

Most of us dream every night, yet we tend to forget our dreams when we wake up. We rarely record our dreams or stop to consider what they mean, yet our dreams can enrich our lives in many ways:

- ◆ They can help us to understand problems in our everyday living and to find a way forward when we don't know which direction to take.
- ◆ They can give us new insights about our intimate relationships and our emotional difficulties.
- ◆ They can unlock our imagination and help us to become more creative.
- ◆ They can show us the gateway to what Jung called 'the collective unconscious' – the deepest layer of the unconscious which extends beyond the individual psyche.

In this book I will show you how to remember some of your dreams and record them in a special dream journal. You can then begin to explore your dreams and gain understanding of the world of dream symbolism. As you explore your dreams you may find that they act like mirrors, showing you hidden aspects of your self and helping you to achieve healing and balance in your life. Your dreams have meanings that are unique to you, so I will also show you how to begin creating your own dream dictionary. You may eventually decide to form a dream group with some friends, or join an online dream group, working together with like-minded people to increase your dream power and understanding.

Our dreams are magical and mysterious. They allow us to ignore the normal rules of time and space, travelling in an instant to distant places, even ones we have never visited physically. We can travel forwards and backwards in time, do battle with scary monsters and change into other people or beings – in fact, anything is possible.

I would like to thank Jenny Fishpool for providing the beautiful illustrations.

At the end of the book you will find a short dream dictionary, some suggestions for further reading and a glossary. Words listed in the glossary are highlighted in bold type when they first appear in the chapters.

I hope you enjoy reading the book and that you find your visits to the dream world as fascinating and productive as I have myself.

Ruth Snowden

Learning about dreams   1

LOOKING AT WHY WE DREAM

Nearly all of us dream, yet nobody has fully explained why. People have always been fascinated by their own dreams, and have tended to believe that they convey meaningful messages. It does not seem likely that they could simply be irrelevant by-products of the sleeping brain, as some have suggested. If people are deliberately deprived of dreaming sleep, they soon get irritable and find it hard to concentrate. They will then catch up on dreams as soon as they can by dreaming more than usual. This suggests that dreams are certainly necessary to us in some way – but why?

Various explanations have been put forward as to why we dream:

- One theory is that a dream is simply a sign that the sleeping brain is ticking over and interpreting signals coming in from the outside, such as the sound of a dripping tap. This theory hardly seems adequate to explain our more involved dreams.
- Another theory suggests that dreams are a bit like information processing going on in a computer: they are the brain's way of sorting out what has happened in our waking life. So while we are asleep, useful information can be processed and stored and the rest is then forgotten. According to this theory, the brain will grapple with ideas and solve problems while we are asleep.
- Dreams could be a form of wish fulfilment, where we can fantasise about what we cannot have, or do, in waking life. This

idea was put forward by Sigmund Freud – more about him later in the chapter.

♦ Yet another theory is that dreams are a kind of internal psychotherapy process, where emotions and problems can be explored in a safe, inner environment.

It is probably true to say that we dream for all these reasons and more. Dreams do seem to help us to process information and also to explore our emotional needs. When we are asleep the conscious brain relaxes its control and the **unconscious** brain takes over, sorting out ideas and feelings that are normally pushed to the back of our mind while we are awake.

LEARNING ABOUT DREAM THEORIES

Dreams in ancient cultures

People have been fascinated by their dreams for thousands of years. Wisdom and healing were often achieved by entering a trance, or travelling through the realm of dreams. Let's have a look at just a few of the ideas that our ancestors had about dreams.

The Australian Aboriginals

The Aboriginal culture of Australia is one of the oldest on earth and some of their ancient knowledge has survived to the present day. Dreams are often seen as memories of, or doorways to, the Dream Time – an endless spiritual time that existed even before the material world was created. There is a sense of oneness and wholeness, where past and present, spirit and human, are joined: the dream world and the everyday world are not seen as separate. Some of these ideas are related to Jung's idea of the **collective unconscious** – see below.

The Egyptians

The Egyptians were very interested in dreams and wrote them down on papyrus. Dreams were often seen as messages from the gods, and people tended to 'incubate' dreams by sleeping in special shrines or temples, such as the temple at Memphis.

The Greeks and Romans

The Greeks and Romans also followed the idea of consulting the gods through dream incubation and often prepared themselves with special rituals involving fasting and animal sacrifices. The great thinker, Aristotle, said that dreams of sickness could often point to trouble brewing in the physical body – a view still current today.

Dreams in Biblical times

Dreams are mentioned throughout the Bible and were often thought to represent divine messages. Bad dreams, on the other hand, were seen as communications from evil spirits. Dreams were often seen as being prophetic – for example, Joseph used one of the Pharaoh's dreams to predict seven years of famine followed by seven years of plenty in Egypt.

What the psychologists say

Over the last century or so, many psychologists have made a serious study of dreams. One of the pioneers in this field of research was Sigmund Freud.

Sigmund Freud (1856–1939)

Freud's work is very important because he was the first person to try to understand how the unconscious works. He said that the unconscious mind contains everything we are not directly aware of in our normal waking life – not only dreams, but also memories, suppressed feelings and urges, as well as innate biological drives and instincts. He believed that these unconscious conflicts and processes affected our waking lives in very important ways.

Freud believed that dreams were manifestations of repressed desires and conflicts; these were usually sexual in nature and arose very early in childhood. According to Freud, the mind heavily censors such ideas, and therefore much of the dream appears in symbolic form, thus masking the true meaning of the dream and allowing the dreamer to carry on sleeping peacefully. Modern psychologists do not tend to agree with this idea – the symbolic imagery in dreams is usually seen as the natural 'picture language' of the sleeping brain.

Freud developed a technique of **free association**, which he used when interpreting his patients' dreams. The patient was simply encouraged to follow trains of thought, beginning with a symbol that appeared in the dream. For example, train – tunnel – entry – sex. This technique can occasionally be useful if you are stuck with a symbol which appears to make no sense.

Carl Jung (1875–1961)

Freud was initially Jung's mentor and Jung built on his work, but eventually Jung developed theories of his own that were very different from Freud's. Freud tended to ascribe fixed meanings to a lot of dream symbols, whereas to Jung many symbols had meanings that were only relevant to the dreamer. He also broke away from Freud's great emphasis on all dreams being about sexual conflicts. Whereas Freud tended to view the unconscious as a mere dumping ground for suppressed ideas, Jung believed that it was infinitely powerful and mysterious. He said that our dreams are of great importance, and that we should meditate upon their meaning until they make sense to us. Jung found that many of his patients who were depressed or disturbed were not in touch with their unconscious. As a result of this, he claimed that we ignore the unconscious messages from dreams at our peril.

Jung often encouraged people to explore dreams as parts of a series, rather than simply looking at individual dreams. He was interested in the way a series of dreams would develop a theme which was important for the personal growth of the dreamer. He also developed the idea of **archetypes** – recurring patterns of thinking shared by all cultures. These emerge from a universal, ancestral **psyche** which he called the collective unconscious. Archetypes represent universally recognisable experiences: for example, people all over the world would understand the idea of motherhood, so the mother is an example of an archetypal figure. Archetypal ideas may also involve inanimate things, such as the sun or water. We will look at archetypes in greater depth later on.

You can learn more about Freud and Jung's fascinating ideas in other books by Ruth Snowden – see Further Reading at the end of the book.

Calvin S. Hall (1909–85)

Hall's work made dream analysis less mysterious and more available to ordinary people. He collected thousands of dreams from people all over the world, discovering many common recurring patterns and categories. He also found individual differences in dream content, relating to people's personal experiences, beliefs and concerns. Hall believed that symbols appearing in dreams were directly expressed visual representations of emotions and thoughts – they were not disguised so that the dreamer could not recognise them, as Freud had maintained.

Modern ideas

Therapists who work with dreams today usually encourage people to find their own interpretations of their dreams. Dreams are often seen as a way of expressing suppressed hopes and feelings. The unconscious mind is bringing problems to the surface in order to help us to confront them and sort them out. Symbolism in the dream is very important, and so is the emotional content. Usually dreams are seen as being relevant to the life of the dreamer at the present time, rather than harking back to childhood.

FORGETTING OUR DREAMS

Although our dreams are important, we tend to forget most, if not all, of their content when we wake up. There may be several reasons for this:

♦ The time factor. Our dreams take up approximately a quarter of our sleeping time. That is roughly two hours a night. If we were to remember them all, it would take up a great deal of our waking hours.

♦ We are normally too busy getting on with our waking life to bother thinking about our dreams. Introverted people, who

Fig 1   Common dream symbols

spend more time analysing their thoughts, tend to recall more dreams than extroverts do.

♦ If the information processing theory about dreams were correct, then it would be logical that we forget the content of dreams that our brain has labelled as useless information.

♦ We may also forget dreams that have a high emotional content, particularly if we are not comfortable with our inner feelings. Often, however, these are dreams that can be very valuable to us, pointing out where our conflicts lie.

EXPLORING SLEEP PATTERNS

Electrical rhythms in the brain

Scientists have found out a lot about the electrical rhythms in the brain by wiring people up to electronic measuring devices. Our brain rhythm alters according to different states of consciousness. Each type of brainwave is referred to by a different letter of the Greek alphabet:

♦ *Beta.* This is the normal rhythm of the brain while we are fully awake.

♦ *Alpha.* This is a slower rhythm, which appears when we are relaxed and drowsy. For example, it appears when we are listening to music, daydreaming or relaxing in the bath.

♦ *Theta.* As we fall asleep the brain goes into this rhythm, which is even slower than alpha.

♦ *Delta.* This is the slowest rhythm of all and it appears when we are deeply asleep or anaesthetised. It can also appear in the deep meditation states achieved by yogis.

REM sleep

During sleep the brain also shows periods of activity connected with rapid eye movements, and a rapid, low-voltage brain rhythm. These periods are called REM sleep (short for Rapid Eye Movement sleep). Most human adults are in REM sleep for 20–25% of the time they are asleep. Research has shown that many of our memorable dreams occur during this phase of sleep. If you have dogs, you will have noticed them twitching and maybe woofing faintly while they are in REM sleep, which suggests that they may be dreaming. Recent research suggests that we dream during other sleep phases as well as during REM sleep.

REM sleep in humans begins about 90 minutes after we fall asleep. The brain waves speed up, heart rate and breathing increase, and blood pressure goes up. Although the brain is very active during REM sleep, the muscles are very relaxed – in fact, the person may be almost unable to move. (One theory suggests that this is so that we do not physically act out our dreams, because this could be dangerous.) There may however be twitching, muttering or even talking, and a person's eyes may be seen moving under the (usually!) closed eyelids. The REM phase occurs in roughly 90-minute cycles throughout the sleep period – usually four or five times during the course of a night. In between comes the deeper, calmer non-REM sleep.

THINKING IN SYMBOLS

Dreams are produced by our unconscious mind, which seems to think very much in symbols, rather than in language. So the dreams appear as pictures, which often build up into a kind of story. The symbols in a dream may mean very different things to different people.

Erich Fromm (1900–80)

Fromm was another psychologist who was interested in dreams and he identified three types of dream symbol:

♦ *Accidental* symbols, which have a personal, individual meaning.
♦ *Conventional* symbols, which tend to have a similar meaning for many people. For example, a car could represent a journey.
♦ *Universal* symbols, which have meaning common to all humans. For example, the sun represents light and warmth. This is the same idea as Jung's archetypes.

A symbol that appears in your dream might fit into any of these categories. If you are stuck with what a symbol means to you, then it may be helpful to consider the more universal meanings. Try to begin taking note of symbols that appear in your dreams. Some of them may appear quite often, in which case they are important to you in some way. Symbols do not have to be objects. Colours, numbers, seasons and characters in your dream may all be symbolic in some way. For example, perhaps you dream that it is autumn – is something coming to an end in your life?

Have a look at the dream symbols illustrated in Figure 1. See if you can think of a personal meaning, a common meaning and a universal meaning for each symbol. Some examples of how to do this are shown in the table below:

Symbol	Personal meaning	Common meaning	Universal meaning
Sun	Summer holiday in Malta	Strength, leadership	Light, growth, warmth
Cat	My cat I had as a child	Feminine qualities, independent nature	Not known in all societies

If you begin to take notice of the symbols that surround you in everyday life, it will help a great deal when you begin to explore your dreams. By thinking about symbols in this way you can begin to understand how a symbol may mean different things to different dreamers, and what particular symbols may mean to you.

LISTENING TO YOUR DREAMS

Every night our dreams can take us on a fascinating inner journey. When you begin to take an interest in your dreams, recording them in your special journal as described in the next chapter, you will probably find that they become more and more interesting and informative. It's a bit like setting up a dialogue with your own unconscious mind. If we listen to the dream messages from our unconscious, they can help us in all sorts of ways. We will look at all these areas in more detail during the course of the book, but meanwhile, here is a brief survey of some of the benefits you may discover.

Some benefits of exploring your dreams

Unearthing hidden conflicts

Dreams can help us to identify areas of hidden conflict and worry which we have not confronted in waking life: sometimes they offer solutions to these problems. As an example, perhaps you dream of your boss as a pig, who gobbles up your lunchtime sandwiches. This dream could be telling you that you feel that your boss is rude and overbearing. We often suppress such knowledge for the sake of peace, but sometimes it is time to speak out.

Showing the way forward

Sometimes our dreams can work as signposts, which point out to us the best direction to take next on our life's journey. Dreams of this type often involve journeys and methods of transport. For example, perhaps you dream that you are driving very fast down a steep hill. This dream might mean that things are difficult for you at the moment – the message could be to slow down and take better control of your life.

Personal relationships

Dreams often give us deeper insights into our personal relationships, making us look at our true feelings and emotions. For example, perhaps you dream that your partner falls off a cliff. This could be wish fulfilment! Or maybe your relationship is not as good as you think it is – your unconscious might be warning you that you may lose your partner if you don't do something about it soon.

Health problems

Through dreams our bodies may warn us about potential health problems: they may also point us towards ways of healing. Supposing you dream all your teeth are falling out. When did you last visit your dentist for a check-up? Your unconscious may be giving you a gentle prompt.

Creativity

Our dreams can help us to become more creative, perhaps with art or story-telling, or maybe giving us ideas for a fantastic new garden layout or other creative project. Simply working with your dreams and the symbols they present can help you to open the door to fascinating creative ideas. Dreams have often acted as inspiration for writers and artists – William Blake, Salvador Dali, Robert Louis Stevenson and Mary Shelley, to name but a few.

Redon (1840–1916) and Goya (1746–1828) both used dream-like symbolism in their art. The spider in Figure 1 is based on Redon's *Smiling Spider*, and Figure 10 is based on Goya's work *The Sleep of Reason Produces Monsters*.

Problem solving
Sometimes dreams can give us fresh insights into puzzling problems, from something as mundane as a baffling crossword clue to major scientific breakthroughs.

Messages about other people
Dreams may contain messages about other people: perhaps ways in which we could help them – or warnings to avoid them! For example, if you suddenly dream that an old school friend is in trouble, try contacting him or her the next day. The unconscious mind is often sensitive to subtle messages that our waking minds may overlook.

Spiritual insights
At a deeper level, our dreams sometimes connect us to archetypal energies and the deeper, spiritual layers of the psyche. These are what Jung called 'big dreams'. These dreams may put us in touch with spirit guides, or inner gurus, or, at a simpler level, they may us tell what our soul is craving – for example, solitude or more contact with nature.

What lies ahead
Dreams can even predict the future! This kind of dream, the 'predictive dream', is one of the most intriguing of all (more on these later). One of the benefits of keeping a dream diary is that you can sometimes read back and spot strange predictive dreams that have come to pass later on, often in uncannily accurate ways. The unconscious is deeply mysterious and full of surprises!

MEETING SOME DREAM EXPLORERS

From time to time we will take a look at the lives of three imaginary dream explorers. These may help you to understand how people's dreams can offer them different personal insights and creative inspirations.

SARAH
Sarah is married, with a grown-up daughter called Nicola. She has worked part-time for many years as an assistant in a shoe shop. She would like to find a job that would give her more interest in life, but she doesn't know how to go about doing this. Her husband Mike is a bit of a couch potato; he works as a foreman at a local factory.

JAMES
James works with computers in an engineering company. He is rather bored with his work and feels that it does not really make full use of his abilities. He is single, having had several long-term relationships in the past, but has never been married. At the moment he is not in a relationship, but he feels that he would like to settle down and have a family, if only he could find the right woman.

JO
Jo is divorced, with two children under ten. The younger one has now started school and Jo has managed to get a part-time job working as a nursery nurse in order to help make ends meet. She is always on the go and never seems to have any time to herself. She would like to be able to go back to college and gain some better qualifications.

QUESTIONS AND ANSWERS

What if I don't dream?
Psychologists now believe that we probably all dream. It is just that some of us find it hard to remember our dreams. As you read through the book you will find suggestions which may help you to recall some of your dreams.

Do we dream in colour?

There is a great deal of uncertainty and dispute about this. Many of us definitely do dream in colour. It seems odd that we should dream in black and white when our normal waking world is perceived in colour. Interestingly, surveys have shown that since black-and-white TV became a thing of the past, more people now report dreaming in colour.

Is it safe to work with my dreams?

Our dreams can be very beneficial to us in developing self-awareness and creativity, so it is a pity not to take notice of them. Some people feel wary of delving into their unconscious, for fear they will uncover something unpleasant. However, writing our dreams down, working with them and talking about them often makes them less powerful and frightening. The process can be a very healing one, allowing us to let go of the past and live more fully in the present. Occasionally people may uncover something that they cannot deal with alone. If you become really disturbed by any of your dreams, you should seek professional help. Never feel afraid or ashamed to do this.

CHECKLIST

The checklist sections throughout the book will help to sum up what you have learned in each chapter and suggest dream-related activities that you might like to do. You might also like to use some of these ideas to inspire shared activities in a dream group (see Chapter 10).

♦ If you are interested in finding out more about dream theories and research, then why not check out current articles online? Your local library may also be a good source of interesting material, and might be able to help put you in touch with like-minded people as well. There are suggestions about further reading at the end the book.

♦ If you fancy working alongside other people, there are many interesting networking websites and discussion groups online. Or you might want to start your own dream group, either online or in your local neighbourhood.

♦ Begin to notice how symbols occur in your dreams. Think about whether they have a meaning that is personal to you alone, or a more commonly understood meaning – or a combination of both.

♦ Think about what you would like to gain from studying your dreams. Make a list of the benefits that you hope will come to you. Are there particular problem areas in your life that you feel you could begin to work on? Would you like to begin using your dreams to stimulate your creativity? If so, in which areas?

Preparing for dreams

2

LEARNING TO RELAX

Making a bedtime ritual

You will have more success with dreamwork if you learn to relax fully before actually settling to sleep. A bedtime ritual is very helpful. Your own ritual will be a very individual one, but some of the following ideas may appeal to you:

♦ Keep to a fairly regular bedtime.
♦ Have a relaxing bath before bed.
♦ Wind down with a good book, a favourite TV programme, or a crossword or other puzzle.
♦ Have a warm drink.
♦ Share some special time with your partner, if you have one.
♦ Follow an evening prayer routine or meditation appropriate to your religion or spiritual path.
♦ Listen to music or to a relaxing CD. There are CDs available to help you to relax – ask at your local complementary health centre or health food shop, or search online.

No doubt you will be able to add other ideas of your own to this list. The important thing is to establish a routine that signals to your body that it is time to wind down and prepare for sleep.

Enjoying a relaxing bath

Bathtime can be a great way to unwind at the end of a busy or stressful day. Make sure the water is nice and warm, but not too hot.

Using aromatherapy oils

Aromatherapy oils in the bath can help you to relax and also help to relieve aches and pains, which may keep you awake. Many ready-mixed bath oils are available on the market. Experiment with these until you find one that suits you. Pure **essential oils** are available from chemists and health food shops in small dropper bottles. You can also find stockists online. These oils are very concentrated, so it is important to add no more than 7–8 drops to your bath water. For children, no more than two drops should be added. Stir the water well to disperse the drops.

Essential oils act directly on your skin and also in the vapour, which you inhale from your bath. Take care with stronger oils such as mint and thyme – these may cause skin irritation. Check with your retailer or therapist about recommended uses, and if possible obtain a good book on aromatherapy. If you find that you are sensitive to a particular oil, then stop using it.

- *Lavender* is a very safe oil for most people, helpful for tension, tiredness and depression.
- *Eucalyptus* is a good decongestant if you have a cold. It soothes muscular aches and pains.
- *Jasmine* is a good oil to use if you feel stressed or tired. It is uplifting for the spirits and also helps dry skin and PMT.
- *Sandalwood* is sensual and relaxing, very good for insomnia.

Lighting colourful candles

Another relaxing idea is to bathe by candlelight. Choose a safe candle-holder and place it somewhere where it cannot set light to curtains, etc., just in case you become drowsy. You can switch off the electric light if you wish, and lie back in the warm, cosy glow. Different-coloured candles can be used to help you in different ways:

- Red – energising and stimulating.
- Orange – cheering and good for low self-esteem.
- Yellow – mentally stimulating and refreshing.
- Green – healing, relaxing and peaceful.

+ Blue – calming and makes you feel serene.
+ Purple – spiritually uplifting, good for meditating by.
+ Pink – cosy and relaxing, soft and feminine.
+ Black – imagine the black candle absorbing negativity.
+ Gold or silver – for special occasions.

Bedtime drinks and snacks

It is not a good idea to have a heavy meal soon before going to bed. This can interfere with sleep patterns and cause indigestion. On the other hand, if you are really hungry then that can keep you awake too. The answer is to have a snack such as a couple of plain biscuits. If you are OK drinking milk, then milky drinks can help you to relax, but avoid tea and coffee last thing, because the caffeine in them may keep you awake.

Making herbal teas

There are various herbal teas which can aid restful sleep and are available from supermarkets and health food shops, in teabags, ready for you to use.

+ **Camomile** is good for over-excitement and nervous stomach problems.
+ **Valerian** is a potent tranquilliser and mild painkiller. It smells horrid, but there are teas available that have valerian mixed with other herbs.
+ **Lemon balm** is refreshing, and a good restorative for the nervous system.
+ **Hops** are good for insomnia, but they must be fresh ones. Put two teaspoons in a cup of boiling water and let it stand for five minutes to brew.

As with the essential oils, discontinue use if you find that you are sensitive to any of these herbs.

Relaxation techniques

Any good book on yoga will give you exercises to do that will help you to relax and unwind. These may include asanas, which are yoga postures, mudras, which are exercises done with special hand positions, and pranayama, or working with the breath. There are many other relaxation methods and the market is full of good books and CDs on self-hypnosis and relaxation, so if you are having trouble relaxing, visit your local library, explore a good bookshop, or trawl the internet to come up with helpful ideas.

REMEMBERING YOUR DREAMS

Sleep studies show that we all have periods of REM sleep, which is the phase of sleep when many dreams occur. It therefore seems likely that we all dream, and yet some of us can never recall any dreams. Most people have had the frustrating experience of knowing that they have just had a dream, only to find it slipping away as soon as they are fully awake. Very often the dreams we do recall are those which are more vivid and meaningful to us in some way. However, it is possible to increase your dream recall considerably, even if you are one of those who are convinced that they never dream. The trick is to get through to your unconscious mind that you are interested in your dreams and wish to recall them.

Catching your dream before it slips away

When you wake up in the morning, try to remember your dreams before you move or stretch your limbs. Laboratory research on dreaming has shown that any movement can impair dream recall. Once you begin to move, your active mind gets into gear too.

Talking about your dream

If you are able to share your dream with someone as soon as you wake up, it often helps you to piece together the fragments. It will also stimulate you to remember parts that you would have otherwise forgotten.

Doodling

If you cannot recall any dreams at all, try doodling on a blank piece of paper. This can sometimes trigger a dream recall.

Observing your mood

Another useful trigger can be simply to observe what sort of mood you are in when you wake up. Sometimes the dream mood carries over for a few minutes after you wake.

Thinking positively

We tend to block our recall of dreams in various ways:

♦ By thinking that our dreams are meaningless or unimportant.
♦ By worrying that traumatic events from the past may return to haunt our dreams.
♦ By being too active and busy all day and not allowing time for reflection.
♦ For fear that we are not ready to be shown current events and relationships in their true light.
♦ For fear that we may have a nightmare, or somehow get too involved in our dreams.

These are all negative attitudes that we need to work through before we can be relaxed about dream recall. One good way to do this is by using positive **affirmations**. An affirmation is a positive statement about the way you want things to be. It is a gentle way of telling yourself that you feel in control.

Using affirmations

When you are nicely warm and relaxed in bed, try one of the following affirmations just before settling to sleep. It will help you to concentrate on your desire to recall your dreams.

♦ I allow myself to recall my dreams and explore their meanings.
♦ I am ready to listen to the wisdom in my dreams.
♦ I will remember dreams that are important to my life at the moment.
♦ I am relaxed and will remember my dreams easily.

You may prefer to make up your own affirmation. Experiment until you find one that is suitable for you.

MAKING A DREAM JOURNAL

Preparing your journal

Begin straight away to keep a notepad and pen, or a small recording device, beside your bed. Then you can record your dreams as soon as you wake up, before they escape. It will also act as another little reminder to your unconscious mind, saying 'I am ready to record my dreams'.

Buy a good A4 exercise book with a hard cover. This is your dream journal. If you want to, you can personalise it by sticking interesting pictures on the cover. Use images that you find particularly interesting or dream like. Soothing images such as soft white clouds in a blue sky or a beautiful seascape would be good. Make your dream journal something special that you can treasure. Make it clear to friends and family that your dream journal is private unless you choose to share a dream. Otherwise you will feel inhibited about writing down some of your wilder and ruder dreams on paper!

Writing down your dreams

If you want to catch any dreams that you recall in the middle of the night, it may be a good idea to keep a torch by the bed. A few quick notes may remind you of your dream in the morning and the torch will save you putting the main light on. If you find that this disturbs you too much and prevents you from getting back to sleep, it is probably best to record only the morning dreams. Try not to use an alarm to wake you up, because this can interfere with your dream recall.

Have a look at the sample page from Jo's dream journal in Figure 2 to see how to set out your pages. At the top of the page write the date and your location at the time of having the dream. Then write down your dream in as much detail as you can remember. Include everything, even if it does not feel like a 'real part' of the original dream. Even dream fragments can be important, so write those down too. It helps always to write your dream down using the present tense, as if it is happening now, for example, 'I am walking along a dark road carrying a tiny lantern. A storm is brewing and the branches of the trees are moving eerily.' This makes your dream more alive and real.

When you have written down as much of your dream as you can remember, write these headings underneath it:

◆ **Feelings**. Write down any emotions associated with your dream, such as fear, anger or frustration.
◆ **Colours**. Take note of any colours that seemed to have special significance, or which are out of place, for example red swans.
◆ **Theme**. Can you pick out a main theme in your dream? For example, running away or flying. Is it a recurring theme in your dreams?
◆ **Symbols**. Write down the main objects that appear in the dream. For example, a car, a tree, a hen and so on.
◆ **Words**. Write down any words that seemed to be important in the dream.
◆ **Setting.** Where did your dream take place?
◆ **People.** Who are the main characters in your dream?
◆ **Other notes**. Make a note of anything else which seems important. For example, numbers, scents and sounds, season of the year and so on.

Once you have jotted down notes under all your headings, make a final section for your analysis of the dream. Allow plenty of space for this, as you may find that you want to add more to it at a later date. We will look at dream analysis in more detail later in the book. Use a fresh page for each new dream. When you have finished recording your dream, think of a suitable title for it, and put this at the top of the page. Then you can number the pages and make an index at the back of the book for your dream journal.

ENCOURAGING MORE DREAMS

There are various techniques you can use in order to encourage more dreams to appear. Once you have tried some of the ones described, you will probably find that you can make new ideas of your own.

Date: 10.02.11   *Title:* Marshmallow dream   *Location:* Home

I am in a huge room like a school canteen. Three small boys are constructing something using bricks, toy cars and marshmallows. I eat a white marshmallow and then a pink one. The children have an aluminium mould for making more marshmallows. When nobody is looking I steal this and take it outside because it contains a yellow marshmallow that I want to eat. I feel very guilty. I am just finishing this marshmallow when the boys come out to look for the mould. One of them produces some yellow marshmallow stuff from behind my ear and stuffs it into my mouth.

Feelings: guilt and greed

Colours: pink, white and yellow (an odd colour for a marshmallow)

Theme: stealing something

Symbols: toys, sweets, mould

Words: none

Setting: school canteen

People: self, small boys

Other notes: body symbols: ear and mouth

Fig 2   A sample page from Jo's dream journal

Making herbal sachets

We have already discussed the qualities of certain herbs when used in the form of herbal drinks or as oils in the bath. You can also use herbs to stuff a small scented sachet, which you can keep under your pillow. Make this sachet from a scrap of silk, wool or cotton and stuff it with any of the herbs mentioned previously, which aid relaxation. You could also try some of the following:

♦ *Mugwort* has a smell which is reputed to aid dream recall and is also supposed to induce prophetic dreams.
♦ *Rose* has a familiar relaxing and comforting smell. Like mugwort, it is reputed to bring prophetic dreams, particularly to do with love.
♦ *Rosemary* is supposed to be particularly useful in warding off nightmares and bringing restful sleep. It is a good herb to use if you are looking for the answer to a particular question.

Making a dream-catcher

This is a Native American idea. The **dream-catcher** is a net woven on a round frame and usually decorated with beads and feathers. It is hung above the bed of the sleeper. There are different theories about how it is supposed to work, but generally the idea is that the net catches the bad dreams, which then evaporate with the first rays of the morning sun. Good dreams drift down to the sleeper below. Other dream-catchers have a central hole to let the bad dreams escape and store the good ones in the net – it's up to you how you choose to see it.

It is satisfying to make your own dream-catcher, and this is another way of signalling your interest in dreams to your unconscious mind. You can make the hoop easily from florist's wire or willow twigs bent into shape and covered with silk or raffia. Weave your net with silk or sparkly thread and decorate your dream-catcher as you wish. Children love to have a dream-catcher above their bed.

Fig 3   A dream-catcher

Here are a few suggestions for decorations for your dream-catcher:

♦ shells or feathers
♦ beads or crystals
♦ tiny objects representing loved ones
♦ a special animal to be your spirit guide in the dream world, for example a cat, dragon, eagle or whatever animal means something to you.
♦ slips of card with titles of previous dreams, for example *magical wooden bowl* or *shop full of black-and-white cats*.

The important thing is to have fun making your dream-catcher and make it into something that is personal and special to yourself. It doesn't matter if the end result is not very artistic – it will still have powerful energy!

Meeting your dream guide

This is a useful idea if you have a good visual imagination. When you are settled in bed, close your eyes and relax. Then imagine that you are walking in a beautiful wood, along the seashore or any other place that you find peaceful and relaxing. Take time to explore your surroundings and enjoy all the things you see and hear. In this special place you will meet your dream guide. It may be a human being that you meet, or some kind of animal or bird.

Once you get to know your dream guide, you can call upon his or her assistance whenever you wish. Your guide may help you to remember your dreams and also to incubate dreams (see Chapter 9), which may help you with specific issues. You may find your guide begins to appear in your dreams as well as in waking visualisations. If so, take special note of those dreams. Many Native American people used dream guides in this way.

Using a dream stone

Gemstones and crystals have been important to human beings for thousands of years. You can choose any stone which attracts you as your special aid. Keep it under your pillow when you go to sleep. Before you drift off, hold the stone in your hand and ask for its assistance. Again, it is your own positive intention which is at work here – different stones can encourage us to work with different energies, so find one that resonates with you:

- ♦ *Moonstone* can help with dreams connected with emotional problems.
- ♦ *Amethyst* is calming and balancing, useful if you suffer from nightmares or insomnia.
- ♦ *Quartz crystal* can help you with problem solving. Think of the expression 'crystal clear' to remind you what this stone's special energy is.
- ♦ *Carnelian* is useful in connection with health and dietary problems.
- ♦ *Lapis lazuli* is a good stone to use for problems related to children, or your **inner child** (see Chapter 6).

JO FINDS A LITTLE TIME FOR HERSELF
Jo is worried about finding enough time first thing in the morning to write down her dreams, because the children are usually awake and demanding attention before she is fully awake. While shopping with her friend Alison, she spots a piece of clear quartz crystal three inches long and feels instantly drawn to it. She decides to buy it and use it as a dream crystal. She explains to the children about her crystal and tells them that when she is holding it in the mornings they must be very quiet. Before long they learn to respect her quiet time and Jo feels better for having a little time for herself.

COPING WITH INSOMNIA

Insomnia can be a real nuisance, but try not to worry about it as this only makes matters worse. It can happen to most of us at times, especially if we are under stress. Try reading for a while, or get up and make a soothing drink. If insomnia becomes more persistent, then consider the following points:

- ♦ Avoid high-protein foods such as cheese and meat shortly before bedtime. These are hard for your stomach to digest and they may keep you awake or even give you nightmares.

♦ Are you under particular stress, or suffering from depression? If so, then talk to a friend, or seek professional help from a doctor or therapist.

♦ Check that there are not too many electrical appliances near your bed. You may be sensitive to the electromagnetic radiation from them.

♦ Avoid drinks containing caffeine, such as tea, coffee and cola. Their effects can linger for several hours. Too much alcohol may also disturb your sleep pattern.

♦ Occasionally insomnia may have another cause. If you are worried, see your doctor.

QUESTIONS AND ANSWERS

Would any kind of stone work as a dream stone?
Any stone which feels right to you is fine, but bear in mind they have different energies. You need to find one that is not too big to slip in your pocket or under your pillow! Some people find a special stone appears at the right time: maybe you will find a small pebble with a face or one with a swirling pattern like a wave. Keep your eyes open when you are out and about.

What if I still can't remember any of my dreams, even when I use the ideas described?
Don't give up! The more motivated you are to remember your dreams, the more likely you are to succeed. Research indicates that introspective people, who naturally focus more on their inner world, are more likely to recall their dreams easily.

What if I don't always have time to record my dreams?
Just relax. Above all, dreamwork should be fun and interesting – a way of getting to know yourself better. If you miss a day or two, or even get fed up with the whole thing for longer periods, don't worry. Your dreams will always be there for you when you are ready to take an interest again.

CHECKLIST

◆ Learn how to unwind properly and find out about which relaxation methods help you the most.

◆ Make yourself a special dream journal and begin to get into the habit of using it. Try to record all the dreams you can, even fragments. They can all give valuable insights.

◆ Explore different ways of helping yourself to recall your dreams and find out what works best for you. Treat yourself to a dream stone, or make yourself a dream-catcher.

◆ When you get a bit more confident, try asking for a dream to help you with a particular problem.

Analysing your dream

3

RELATING DREAMS TO WAKING LIFE

Now that you have begun to collect your dreams in your dream journal, let's have a look at ways in which you can begin to interpret their meaning. The first and most obvious thing to do is to discover whether your dream relates in some way to your everyday waking life at the moment. Dreams often contain symbols or other aspects that relate directly to your current situation.

For example, perhaps you get a letter from your old school, asking you for a donation to support their appeal fund. That night you might dream that you are back in the classroom, struggling with some difficult maths. Or perhaps you go round to a friend's house for coffee and her cat jumps up on your lap. That night you dream that a cat has sauntered in through your own back door and is helping herself to some cream.

There are two main things to look for if your dream seems directly related to your waking experiences.

- The dream may simply refer to an event that happens to be foremost in your mind after your waking day. In this case perhaps your brain is just processing the information and either storing it away for future reference or rejecting it as unimportant.
- The dream may be working with a symbol that has cropped up in your waking life but is also important to you in some deeper way. For example, the school dream may be bringing up old feelings

of insecurity that relate back to a time when you were bullied. In this case the dream is giving you an important message – this is an area of your life that you need to give attention to. The external event has triggered a train of thoughts and feelings in your unconscious.

Have a good look at your dream and see how any of the following aspects of it may be directly related to events in your waking life now:

Location

Have you recently been to the location of your dream? Or perhaps you have seen it on television, or read about it in a book? What associations do you have with the place? How does it make you feel? Try to write down four words in your dream journal that describe your dream location. For example, supposing you dream that you are on a warm, palm-fringed beach. Your four words could be 'sunshine, relax, peace, water'. The beach is evidently a pleasant place, where you would like to be. Perhaps you have recently watched a holiday advert on the television and your unconscious brain has stored this image away in order to remind you that you need a holiday soon.

People

Are you directly involved with any of the characters in your dream at the moment? Or have you seen them around somewhere, or read about them recently? If not, then who do the characters remind you of? Again, try to write down four words to describe each character. For example, you dream about a woman in nurse's uniform. Perhaps your words are 'bossy, strict, caring, efficient'. Have you met anyone like this lately, or could the 'nurse' figure be an aspect of yourself?

Symbols

Have any of the objects in your dream appeared recently in your waking life? Why do you think they could be important to you? For example, you visit a museum and see some large Roman storage jars. That night you dream about storage jars with honey in them. Why have you chosen the symbol of a storage jar – what does it mean to you? In this dream you would also need to think about what honey means to you. Perhaps it could be a symbol of sweetness that you need to find in your life.

Feelings

How did you feel during your dream? Did your emotional state change during the course of the dream? Have you felt like this in real life recently? Very often, if we are going through a period of emotional upheaval, we will have dreams that echo those feelings. These dreams are important, and often hold clues to helping us sort out our problems.

Other aspects

You will discover for yourself other aspects of your dream that relate to your waking life. For example, take note of colours, times, seasons and so on.

Understanding your present situation

Your dream is like a mirror, showing you how you really think and feel. To understand your dreams is to understand yourself better. A very good way of beginning this process of understanding is to look at your dreams and see ways in which they relate directly to your present situation.

LOOKING AT EMOTIONS

Sometimes the way we feel during a dream is even more important than the visual content of the dream. Read back through your dream and try to imagine you are replaying the dream, like watching a film. How do you feel during the dream? Was there one particular emotion, or did your feelings change during the course of the dream? Write down anything that comes into your mind at this stage, even if it seems silly or totally unconnected to the original dream. Everything you write down in your dream journal will be important to you. Listed below are some key emotions to look out for in your dream:

- ◆ fear
- ◆ joy
- ◆ anger
- ◆ love
- ◆ embarrassment
- ◆ anxiety

How many more can you think of? Try to list some more and write them down in the front of your dream journal, so that you can refer to the list when you need to. As you collect more dreams you will begin to notice that certain emotions come up time and time again. These are the ones that you need to be dealing with and exploring in your waking life. It may surprise you to find out which emotions are appearing in your dreams. If they are feelings that you did not expect to find, then you should ask yourself if for some reason you are actually suppressing them in waking life.

Feeling unusual emotions

Make special note of emotions that appear odd or out of place in some way, for example, hateful feelings towards someone whom you normally love. Try to look at these feelings honestly and objectively, and see if you can discover a hidden message there for yourself. For example, perhaps there is anger hidden away, which you dare not confront for fear of disturbing your comfortable existence?

Be careful not to over-react when exploring in this way. Sometimes inappropriate emotions in dreams do appear to be just that! Perhaps you have a passionate sex dream about your boss, for example, whereas in waking life you genuinely don't feel that way. Our unconscious occasionally seems to develop a silly sense of humour, as if it were playing games with us, or trying out bizarre ideas just for a change. Or maybe the message that it is trying to put across is something rather different. In this instance the message might not be 'I am in love with my boss', but rather 'I need to lighten up a bit and take myself less seriously'.

DISCOVERING DREAM SYMBOLS

Another very important aspect of your dream is the **symbols** that it contains. The unconscious brain tends to present ideas to us in symbolic form and the meaning of these symbols is often unique to the dreamer. For example, a cup may represent emotions, psychic ability, gestation or the unconscious; it is also used as a religious symbol; or it might be a personal symbol, reminding you of a special prize that you won in childhood. Refer again to the notes that you have made under your dream in your journal. What particular symbols have you picked out?

Studying Jo's dream symbols

If you look again at the sample page from Jo's dream journal in Chapter 2, you will see that she selects 'toys, sweets and mould' as the symbols in this dream. We will have a look at each of these symbols in turn.

Toys

Toys are generally associated with childhood. There may be a feeling of fun, being frivolous, 'toying with' an idea. Remember, however, that Jo has two small children and works as a nursery nurse. She writes in her dream journal that toys are very much a part of her everyday life. She is constantly tripping over them, quite literally.

Sweets

The marshmallows in the dream are soft and fluffy, as well as good to eat. Jo associates them with spoiling herself and finding the sweet things in life. The colour is important here, however, because some of them are yellow, rather than the usual pink or white. Yellow is the colour often associated with an active mind, being well organised and communicating. Jo thinks that this is very appropriate when she has just started her dream journal. She decides that writing down her dreams is beginning to help her to organise her thoughts. She realises that it is significant that she wants to sneak away from the children to eat her marshmallows – her unconscious seems to be telling her that she needs time alone, away from children.

Mould

Moulds are usually used for making lots of objects of the same shape. Jo feels that this could be to do with the repetitive nature of small children's play. She realises that she often feels stifled by this. She needs to get away – to go outside, as she did in her dream, away from the children and by herself. She is no longer fitting into the 'mould' of mother and carer. In fact, part of her wants to 'break out of the mould'.

Finding your own symbols

After recording your dreams for a while, you will find that certain symbols crop up quite often. These symbols carry an important message for you. For example, supposing you often dream about blocked drains. What do you feel is blocked up in your life? It could be pent-up emotions, or it could be a message about your physical body, telling you that you are blocking your energy in some way. Do you need to talk to somebody about your feelings, or do you need to go on a cleansing diet after spending the winter as a couch potato?

You will find that the symbols which crop up frequently will gradually change over a period of time, as your unconscious brain mulls over fresh problems.

Recurring symbols

It is a curious fact that some symbols which appear in your dreams may crop up in real life as well, or else in books and films. Make a note of these **coincidences** in your dream journal. Maybe you dream about a falcon and the next day you see one flying alongside your car on the way to work. The falcon is sharp-eyed, swift and direct in flight. Does it have a message for you? Try this for yourself and see if you can discover dream symbols and waking symbols that overlap.

We will discuss dream symbols in greater depth in the next chapter. For the time being, just begin to be aware of the symbols that occur in your life and dreams. Consider how almost every aspect of your dream can be seen as a symbol in some way. Not only objects, but also colours, people, places and so on. For example, Jo could just as easily select 'canteen, small boys, bricks, cars' as the symbols in her dream.

FINDING RECURRING PATTERNS

As you begin to build up your dream journal, you will quite likely find that certain themes, or whole dreams, tend to recur. These recurring patterns are showing you aspects of your world which are important to you.

JAMES IS ALWAYS BEING DELAYED

James records a lot of frustrating dreams about trying to get ready for something and being constantly delayed. Usually it is an important meeting, or an interview, which he simply must get to. There are all sorts of trivial annoyances that hold him back every time. His car will not start. He finds that he is still wearing his pyjamas. He notices that his main feelings are of irritation and frustration. He decides that the dreams are related to his feelings about his real-life work.

Recurring themes

If a dream theme occurs over and over again, then it is quite likely that your unconscious is trying to get a message through to you, but you are not picking up the telephone, as it were. You are not listening to the message that is being put across, and so your unconscious is trying to put it across in slightly different forms, but following the same basic theme. Often these are themes that are to do with more deep-seated fears and anxieties, which sometimes, as Freud said, may hark back to when we were younger.

When we are children we acquire beliefs and attitudes which we carry forward into adult life. Sometimes your dreams are telling you that it is time now to have a good look at these beliefs, and perhaps discard ones which are no longer relevant or helpful in your life. For example, maybe you often dream that you are sitting an exam, or that you have failed horribly in an exam. If exams are not actually relevant to your life now, then perhaps you came from a family where it was desperately important to do well at school. Now that your unconscious has brought the theme up, you can begin to look at this belief in a more adult way, and perhaps begin to be easier on yourself.

We will look at some common dream themes in greater depth later on in the book. For the time being, have a look at this list of common themes and see if you can identify with them and perhaps add a few more of your own:

- falling dreams
- dreams where you are being chased
- dreams about water
- dreams about houses, which may or may not be houses you are familiar with
- travel and transport dreams
- dreams about delays and frustrations
- flying dreams
- toilet dreams

When you begin to notice a recurring theme in your dream journal, you may find it helpful to add notes about what has been going on in your life. See if there is an emerging pattern that can be linked to the content of the dreams. For example, every time you go to visit your parents you might have dreams about water, in different forms. Sometimes it may be a raging flood; other times just a small trickling stream. Begin to build up an understanding about what these dreams are trying to tell you.

Recurring dreams

Recurring dreams are especially important because they tend to relate to major issues. As with recurring dream themes, it may be that the conscious mind is not really responding to a message about a life issue. Sometimes exactly the same dream happens over and over again, and sometimes the content varies a little bit – but the dream sequence is always similar. If you have a recurring dream, try to explore it by asking questions such as:

- What message is this dream trying to convey?
- Am I reluctant to hear that message?
- Is the dream about a hidden fear that I would rather not bring out into the open?
- Is it about some hidden aspect of a relationship that I fear to admit?
- Is it about a neglected talent that I know I should make use of?

Sometimes recurring dreams are more mysterious, and they may have a pre-cognitive element. When I was about four I had a terrifying recurring nightmare, in which the whole world had turned into one gigantic factory. I was hugely responsible in this, because I had just picked the last flower, in the last green field. A strange and haunting pre-cognitive dream for a tiny child living in rural Britain, long before globalisation or climate change were ever discussed around me, or even mentioned in the news – we didn't even have a television! How did I *know* about the devastating changes that were to arise in my lifetime?

EXPLORING THE DREAM MESSAGE

There are many ways in which you can begin to unravel the messages hidden within your dreams. Try out all of the methods described below. You will gradually begin to find out which ones work best for you. Usually you will need to use a combination of different methods before you begin to understand your dream. If you still find that you are stuck, then put the dream on one side for a little while. The dream will still be there at the back of your mind and sometimes an event may occur that will give you a flash of insight and you will say to yourself, 'So that was what that dream meant.'

Go through your dream and pick out any symbols that you feel to be important. Don't forget to include colours, numbers, seasons and even words, as well as objects and people. Now, looking at each symbol in turn, write down any ideas which spring to mind as to what you feel that symbol means to you. There are various methods you can use to help you:

Using a dream dictionary
These books can be very helpful in triggering associations in your mind. However, it is important not to think that their interpretation will always be the right one for your own dream. Remember that symbols can mean different things to different people.

Using an ordinary dictionary

Simply look up the word for your symbol in a dictionary or thesaurus. The dictionary definition sometimes gives you a new angle.

Exploring myths and folklore

Some symbols have meanings that are often found in familiar stories, such as **myths** or folktales. Think of a dragon, for instance, who might be greedily sitting on his hoard of gold, isolated from companionship. Or the dragon might instead be a symbol of magical power. Dragons can be good or evil, depending upon the story.

Explaining your dream to someone

Simply describing your dream to a friend or discussing it in a group often helps you to grasp its meaning. As you put the dream into words that other people can understand, you gain sudden fresh insight yourself. You might be describing a ring that appeared in your dream, for example, and then you say to your friend, 'Come to think of it, I had a ring like that when I was about eight.'

Drawing your dream

It doesn't matter whether you think you are good at drawing or not. Seeing your dream as a picture will often give fresh insights. You will probably find that you add extra bits to the picture as you go along, but this doesn't matter, because you are still communicating with your unconscious. Drawing can be a very valuable therapy in itself.

Free associating

This is the method that was used by Freud. Just say any words that come into your head when you say the word for your symbol. See where the train of thought leads you. Try it now with these words, just for practice: *field, elephant, blanket*. Write down your trains of thought in your journal.

First record your dream

Write the dream down in as much detail as possible. Include everything, even if it seems stupid or 'made up'.

Does the dream seem to relate directly to events in your waking life?

♦ Does it seem like 'data processing'?
♦ Or does it seem to have a more symbolic content?

Now work on the symbols in your dream, using any of the following methods:

♦ a dream dictionary
♦ an ordinary dictionary
♦ myths and folklore
♦ explaining your dream to another person
♦ drawing your dream
♦ free association

Now leave your dream alone for a while

♦ You will learn more about your dreams as you read on in the book.
♦ Some dream meanings become clearer after a few days.

Fig 4   Chart to help with dream analysis

QUESTIONS AND ANSWERS

When symbols appear both in dreams and in waking life, is it mere coincidence?

Sometimes it is obviously just a random coincidence, but often we have a powerful feeling that there is more to it. Jung called these meaningful coincidences 'synchronicities' and maintained that the inner and outer worlds are closely connected. It is important to take note of synchronous dream occurrences, because they may lead us to powerful insights.

What if my dream doesn't seem to relate to my waking life?

There could be many different reasons for this. For example, your dream might be related to issues that you are suppressing in some way – have a good look at the imagery and emotions in your dream. Or the dream might be related to issues from your past which are unresolved and maybe surfacing in some way right now. It might even relate to a past life, or to the future – more on these interesting topics later!

What if I cannot understand one of my dream symbols?

Stay with it and mull it over. Sometimes symbols don't seem to mean anything at first. Try drawing your dream, or talking it over with somebody. If it still remains obscure, try asking for another dream to clarify what the previous dream means.

CHECKLIST

- ◆ Practise your dream work by considering the examples in the book and asking questions such as:
  1. In view of his recent dreams, what do you think James might consider doing next in waking life?
  2. Can you think of possible ways Jo could begin to 'break out of the mould'?
- ◆ Take note of ways in which your dreams relate to your everyday life.

◆ Notice how your dreams can uncover deep-seated emotions. Are some of these emotions ones that you would like to work on changing in your life?

◆ Study symbols that crop up, not only in dreams, but also in the world around you. Take particular note of any synchronicities that occur.

◆ Begin to notice the underlying themes that recur in your dreams. Can you figure out why they keep on occurring? Is there anything that you could begin to do to help address any problems or issues that they are pointing to?

4 *Exploring dream symbolism*

UNDERSTANDING ARCHETYPAL FIGURES

Although our dreams are personal conversations with ourselves from our unconscious, there is a lot of common ground in the types of images that we all experience. This shared **imagery** forms what Jung referred to as the **collective unconscious**. Archetypes are the contents of the collective image bank. As you will remember, an archetype is a pattern of experience which is common to all humans. It may appear in many ways, for example as a symbol, an image, a pattern, a feeling, an idea or a person.

It is useful to be aware of archetypes, because they express ideas that many other people can understand. They can provide us with a kind of structure, or 'mind map', drawing on the experience of others who have been there before us. This can help to guide us towards finding out what our dreams are saying. In this section we will look at some of the most common archetypal figures which may crop up in your dreams. Here are some of the more common ones:

victor	child	stranger
male	martyr	warrior
female	fool	priest
priestess	judge	hermit
mother	teacher	traveller
father	monster	baby
victim	bully	boss
nurse	saint	savage

Have a good look through your dream journal and see if you can pick out any characters that could be considered as archetypes. What do you feel those figures might be trying to tell you?

Often an archetype appears as a representation of a part of ourselves, or of another person who is important to us in some way. If you have found archetypes appearing in your dream, try to think who they remind you of:

♦ Are they like your partner in some way?
♦ Do they remind you of one of your parents?
♦ Or do you feel that the figure is mirroring some aspect of your own personality?

Sometimes both things may be true – the archetypal figure is an aspect of yourself and also of another person. The important thing is that archetypes are pointing out to you issues that you need to think about. Perhaps you need to be more like the figure you dream about. Or perhaps that figure is blocking your personal growth in some way. Very often the archetype is pointing out to you a role that you play in life, or a role that would be helpful for you to adopt.

Let's have a look at a few archetypal figures who may appear in your dreams.

Meeting the hermit
The hermit is a solitary figure, but not necessarily lonely. He or she often appears in our dreams when we are going through a period of spiritual growth. The hermit may indicate a need to withdraw for a while and spend time alone, away from the hectic everyday world. The figure is telling you to listen to your inner voice – it has a message for you. Perhaps you are too quick to listen to the advice of others, and are ignoring your own instincts? The hermit may appear in any solitary form – as an actual hermit type, or as a wandering albatross, a monk or nun, or perhaps as the Lady of the Lake. The guru is a similar archetypal figure who may appear in your dreams.

Meeting the warrior

The warrior is an assertive, aggressive character, who is very much in control. He or she is highly trained, efficient, proud and brave. How do you feel about this figure? Does it remind you of somebody that you know, or is it telling you that you need to stop being passive and stand up for your own rights? Do you feel that you would like to be the warrior, or is the figure opposed to you and threatening?

Meeting the monster

The monster is a common dream figure, especially dreaded by children. If one appears in your dreams, then confront it. Write down a really detailed description of it. How do you feel about it now? What aspects of your monster make it frightening? Monsters can be incredibly variable and personal beasts. They range from the grey slimy Crawly Lump my mother dreamed of as a child, to the huge fire-breathing dragon. Remember that we all have monsters that we fear hidden away in dark corners. When your monster puts in an appearance, be glad – your unconscious is telling you that you are ready to face it and drag it out into the daylight.

Balancing male and female

Male archetypal energy is assertive and intentional. The female counterpart is passive and receptive. All of us have both energies within our psyche, but according to our sex and our upbringing, one tends to dominate over the other. In the dream world we may experiment with different gender roles. This may apply to the physical body – for example, a man dreams he has given birth, or a woman dreams she has a penis. We also try out different types of behaviour – for example, a quiet submissive woman dreams she is a Viking warrior, or a macho rugby-playing man turns into a geisha girl.

When we are going through a period of active change in our life rebalancing often needs to occur, so dreams of this sort may arise. The psyche is saying, 'This is what I need – forbidden or not!' Listen to its message. See if you can think of ways of integrating new balance into your life. For example, the quiet woman could do an assertiveness training course, and the rugby player could take up growing roses.

NOTICING DREAM COLOURS

Not everybody is aware of dreaming in colour. For those of us who are, however, the colours can sometimes be very vivid and important. Now and again a certain colour will seem to stand out, and is obviously trying to convey an important message. Each colour has particular energies commonly associated with it (see Figure 5) and each of us also has individual associations with specific colours.

If you want to encourage colours to appear in your dreams, then try this:

♦ Select a colour that appeals to you – let's say bright blue.
♦ Gather some small objects in your chosen colour, for example a flower or a crystal.
♦ Place the objects by your bed and, focusing on them, visualise the colour strongly before settling to sleep, and ask for a dream with that colour in it.

Studies have shown that colours can definitely affect our mood. Pink, for example, is calming and healing, whereas orange is energising. If a colour appears prominently in a dream it may indicate that you need the energy of that particular colour at the moment, or that you are already opening up to changes in your life. Look out especially for colours that seem unusual or out of place, such as a red banana.

Finding your own colour associations

Make a list of colours and write down any associations that spring to mind as you think about each colour. This list will help you when colours appear in your dreams. Use some of the following ideas to help you:

Who wears this colour?
Does your brother always tend to wear blue? Or does the shy retired schoolteacher next door always seem to wear brown?

Colour phrases
Think of any phrases associated with colour, such as 'green with envy', 'red as a beetroot', 'the black night of the soul' or 'in the pink'.

Colour people
There are lots of these in myths, songs and traditional sayings, for example 'lady in red', 'the white goddess' and 'the green man'.

Using your colours
If a colour seems to be sending you a meaningful message in a dream, then try using that colour more in your waking life for a while. Try some of the following ideas:

♦ Light a candle in your chosen colour and sit quietly for a while watching its flame.
♦ Wear something in your chosen colour.
♦ Sometimes colours are sending us a food message. For example, if you dream of green, try eating more salad or green vegetables.
♦ Buy something for your home that has your colour in it, or even redecorate a room with it.

OBSERVING SEASONS AND WEATHER

What do the seasons mean to us?
The seasons of the year have always been very important to human beings. Our ancestors, who lived much closer to the land, were of necessity more in touch with the rhythms of the year. Even in today's artificially controlled environment, the seasons are still deeply rooted in our psyche. As children many of us have known the joy of scrunching through autumn leaves, or lazing in long grass above our heads in the summer.

Colour	Positive aspects	Negative aspects
Red	Energy, health, stimulation, sex, strength, excitement.	Danger, violence, pain, frustration, anger.
Orange	Optimism, openness, health, renewal, warmth.	Arrogance, selfishness, superficiality.
Yellow	Creativity, clarity, imagination, intelligence.	Cowardice, fear, inhibition, anxiety.
Green	Growth, healing, money, grace, peace.	Avarice, envy, selfishness, loneliness.
Blue	Peace, serenity, wisdom, grace, spirituality.	Depression, introversion.
Indigo	Spiritual awakening, meditation, withdrawal.	Becoming too serious or detached.
Violet	Power, cleansing, spiritual and psychic awareness.	Tyranny, spiritual pride.
Black	Instinct, night-time, the unconscious, power.	Fear, depression, death.
White	Purity, cleansing, spirituality, perfection.	Spiritual pride, 'whitewashing'.
Brown	Grounding, nourishment, security, rest.	Dullness, depression, lack of inspiration.
Pink	Healing, love, femininity, gentleness, peace.	Helplessness, over-dependence.

Fig 5   Traditional meanings for colours

Your ideas about the seasons are naturally affected by the part of the world in which you live, so they may differ from the ones described below. The important thing is to recognise that the psyche goes through seasonal cycles of its own throughout our lives. These may be cycles of birth, death, growth, resting and so on. When the season is important in your dream, consider whether this reflects an inner cycle you are passing through at the moment, or need to embark on.

Spring
Spring is usually seen as a time of rebirth, innocence, questioning and insight. It is connected to childhood in the human life cycle. Think of the phrase 'out with the old, in with the new'. Dreams involving spring tend to reflect new growth, new ideas or taking a new direction in life. Perhaps you are thinking of embarking on a new project or conceiving a child.

Summer
Summer is associated with carefree days and easy living. It is the season of abundance, warmth and comfort. Things are going well. It is a time for holidays and parties – the season of sociable get-togethers. It relates to the time of youth, when we are full of energy, vigour and strength. Dreams where summer is prominent may be telling you that the good times are here and projects will succeed.

Autumn
Autumn is about the completion of cycles, and reaping the reward for hard work that was begun earlier. It is a time of harvest, plenty, money and material goods. There is also the idea of storing up good things for future need, with the coming of winter. Dreams about autumn may be telling us that we are nearing the end of a cycle. It is time to assess what we have learned, let go and move on. Autumn corresponds to mature adulthood, and feelings of responsibility and stability.

Winter
Winter is the fallow time, when we turn to contemplation. It is a time of death, rebirth, renewal and planting seeds. The energies are

drawn into the self, for a period of hibernation. It marks the end of a cycle in life. Dreams about winter speak to us of inner awareness and spiritual growth. It corresponds to the season of old age, when the spirit is gradually released from everyday, earthly matters.

Expanding your ideas about the seasons

Drawing the seasons

Try drawing or painting a picture for each of the seasons in the country you live in. It doesn't matter if you don't think you are good at art. The important thing is to find out what your own associations are. What colours do you want to select for each season?

Celebrating the seasons

Make a list of the various celebrations throughout the year, such as Christmas, that occur in your own religion, culture and family. Don't forget to include birthdays. Which is your favourite season? How do you feel when you think about that season? Do you have different feelings about other seasons?

Noticing the weather in dreams

Different weather conditions seem to come up quite frequently in dreams. They often reflect our emotional state.

Rain

Rain usually indicates a period of emotional cleansing. It washes away things that we have finished with, leaving us refreshed. Persistent rain may convey a dismal feeling.

Snow

Snow is pure and white, giving a feeling of freshness. It may indicate a totally new start – a blank sheet.

Ice

Do you feel that something is frozen, at a standstill? Your emotions may be locked inside you, unable to flow. There is also the idea of 'skating on thin ice'.

Wind

Winds tend to blow things away and bring changes into our lives. A lot depends on the strength of the wind in your dream. A tornado or hurricane probably indicates that things are moving too fast, or getting beyond your control.

Storm

Storms are dangerous and threatening. You probably feel vulnerable at the moment, and your surroundings are unpredictable. Look for shelter until your storm has blown itself out.

Cloud and fog

Something is not clear to you at the moment, or perhaps a dark cloud has come into your life and covered up your sun.

Rainbow

This is a happy dream message, which signifies joy and celebrations. Rainbows often appear after a storm.

Sun

This is usually an indication of happiness, success, peace and inner strength.

Flood

Your emotions may be getting totally out of control. Do you feel overwhelmed by something? Or are you suppressing a flood of feeling?

You will be able to add to these ideas for yourself. Take note if the weather seems to change during your dream. For example, perhaps it gets colder or a mist comes down. Use these weather clues for hints as to your true feelings about a situation.

FINDING NUMBERS IN YOUR DREAMS

Sometimes a number seems to assume special significance in a dream. If you are lucky, perhaps it is a winning lottery number! Traditionally numbers do have special associations, so see if any

Number	Positive meaning	Negative meaning
1	New beginnings. Things which are about to happen. Independence and individuality. Determination. Inventions.	Wilfulness, selfishness, loneliness.
2	Partnerships in love or business. Balancing and co-operation. Agreement. Diplomacy.	Duality – being two-faced. Imbalance.
3	Fun and parties. The trinity, or the triple goddess. Mind, body, spirit. Help, harmony and communication. Sharing, enjoyment, friendship and love.	Scattered energy. Over-indulgence.
4	Balance, stability. Four-square. Four-legged animals. Two couples. Team work, organisation, planning, making a solid foundation.	Dull, boring and materialistic. Stuck energy. Reluctance to move on.
5	Changes, expansion and travel. Moving on. The magical pentagram.	Misfortune, failure, loss. Problems and regrets.
6	Harmony. Responsibility and maturity. Comfort, care, compassion, sharing.	Lack of compassion or responsibility. Disharmony.
7	Inner wisdom and magical powers. Solitude, religious thinking and ritual. Great achievement through effort.	Fear and ignorance. Daydreaming and escapism. Evasiveness and sneaky behaviour.
8	Capability, success, attainment. Seeing things in their true light.	Strain, oppression. Inability to make the effort required.
9	Fulfilment, wisdom, achievement. Self-reliance. Personal contentment and maturity.	Loss and having to let go. Loneliness.
10	Completion and success. Satisfaction. End of cycle – a new one is beginning.	Oppression and weariness. Feeling stuck or martyred.

Fig 6   Traditional meanings for numbers

of the ideas in Figure 6 seem to strike a chord. Remember to look for your own number associations too, such as birthdays, your age, your house number or perhaps a number that is lucky for you.

JAMES GOES ON A BOAT TRIP

James dreams that he is taking a journey by boat along a river. He comes to a place where there are two alternative ways to go, so he asks a passer-by for directions. He is told that he can carry on the way he is going, or else he can go 'through the seven locks, up the shining hill'. He decides that the seven locks symbolise something to which he has to find the keys. If he does this he will be able to get 'up the shining hill' – this sounds more interesting than plodding on the way he is going. Researching his dream symbols later, he finds out that seven is traditionally a magical number, but it involves work and effort too. He decides to do some studying at home, with a view to setting up his own business.

PLAYING WITH WORDS

Some people don't dream all that much in picture symbols. They tend to use words a lot and hear things being said to them in their dreams. Sometimes people find that a 'higher being' or mentor figure comes into a dream, to give some profound words of wisdom. Words in dreams are sometimes puns, with a double hidden meaning. This type of symbolism may crop up more in your dreams if you have a particular interest in words. Perhaps your work involves words or languages. Or perhaps you are a keen crossword solver.

JAMES IS NOT ALLOWED THROUGH THE DOORS OF PERCEPTION

James dreams that 'the doors of perception' are in his mother's kitchen. He is not allowed through them, because she says that he is not yet ready. They are secret, hidden by a grille, and James feels that something he needs to know lies beyond them. He feels frustrated and tantalised by this. He knows that his unconscious is almost ready to tell him something, but his waking self feels unprepared and not ready to cope with the revelation.

Quite often the words in a dream seem to carry a very profound meaning, and yet upon waking and writing them down, they seem trivial or meaningless. If this is the case, just go with it, and leave the dream alone for a while. The meaning may become apparent in a few days' time. Sometimes the act of writing the dream down makes the double meaning become clear. It often helps to tell your dream to somebody else, because as you speak the words aloud they reveal their meaning.

For example, perhaps you dream about somebody called Mrs Owen – when you say the name aloud, you realise that in your dream this person 'owes' you some money. The pun or meaningful phrase in your dream may actually be spoken aloud, or it may be presented in a visual form, even though it is a play on words. Dream puns can be very humorous. They are often liberating and cathartic, in the same way as humour is in waking life. Perhaps your pun may be telling you to lighten up a bit and not take yourself so seriously. Look at the funny side for a change.

QUESTIONS AND ANSWERS

What if my ideas about colours, etc. are different from the common ones?
That's fine – always go with your own gut feeling, because this will get you more readily to an understanding of your dream. But bear in mind that widely held associations can be very helpful to look at when you are stuck.

Supposing a number in my dream seems to have sinister meaning?
This is a tricky one. Always look at the dream as a whole, and don't get too hung up on a particular number or symbol. If you remember to do this you will often find an underlying message that will help you forward. And always try to remember that the dream is coming from your own unconscious. Is there any particular reason why you might find this number threatening? Think back to childhood, or a time when you were going through difficulties.

What if a dream voice tells me to do something horrible or dangerous?

Again, always remember that the dream is the voice of your own unconscious. Is the message trying to unblock hidden emotions such as anger and frustration? It is important not to 'act out' on messages like these, but rather take a long hard look at yourself and your entrenched beliefs. If necessary, seek counselling.

CHECKLIST

♦ Relate James's difficulty in going through 'the doors of perception' to your own life. In other words, what do you need to understand better or see more clearly? Make a list of any techniques or ideas which might help you to go through these doors.

♦ Experiment with wearing different colours and notice how they make you feel. Begin to use colours to enrich your life and balance your energies. Do you associate your friends and other people with specific colours? Make a note of when particular colours appear in your dreams.

♦ Play 'Who am I?' with friends. Decide which archetypal figure each of you is most like at the moment. For example, mother, teacher, fool and so on.

♦ If an archetypal figure begins to appear in your dreams, take notice. Try to work out what this figure is telling you about your current situation.

♦ When you record your dreams, look out for extra messages hidden in words and phrases, as well as in visual images.

Seeing your dream as a mirror 5

TALKING TO DREAM CHARACTERS

One of the most powerful ways in which our dreams work is by acting like mirrors. They show us aspects of ourselves that we are not always consciously aware of in waking life. Some dream theorists go so far as to maintain that all the characters who appear in our dreams are in fact different facets of our own personality. It is certainly true that things that we notice and find irritating in other people are often the very things which we wish to deny in our own personality. Freud called this process **projection**, because undesirable aspects of behaviour are projected outwards onto other people.

Dream characters may work in any of the following ways, or even in a combination of more than one of these ways:

- ◆ They may be telling us a few home truths about ourselves.
- ◆ They may be illustrating how we really feel about other people.
- ◆ They sometimes appear to point out aspects of our personality that we feel are lacking.

Pretending to be a dream character

Choose a character from one of your dreams. Now simply pretend that you are that person, and begin to explain what you are doing in the dream. It helps to begin by explaining who you are. Say the words 'I am a grey monster', or 'I am a pirate with a wooden leg' or whoever you happen to be. Don't forget to think about how you feel, as well as what you are doing.

SARAH IS A JUNGLE EXPLORER

Sarah dreams that she is walking through a jungle and she meets an explorer. The explorer is being criticised by a crowd of people, because she has been looking after a group of monkeys and has now left them behind 'on a high peak', overlooking the jungle.

Sarah decides to speak as her dream character: 'I am an explorer. I have had to leave the monkeys behind. It was necessary because I needed to explore deeper into the jungle. They can take care of themselves now – they don't need me all the time. Anyway, they can still see me from where they are.'

What do you think Sarah's dream could mean? Who is the explorer? What could the monkeys represent? Remember that Sarah's daughter is now an adult, and Sarah is trying to work out what to do in the next phase of her life.

Sarah thinks about the explorer in her dream and she begins to see that since Nicola finally left home she has actually reached a stage in her life when she is free to 'explore'. She notices that animals are appearing quite often in her dreams and remembers that as a young girl she always wanted to work with animals. She decides to visit the library and the job centre to see if there are any openings for her.

Changing your viewpoint

An interesting aspect of some dreams is that we actually change personalities halfway through the dream. Sometimes we are even aware of being two characters at once – the actor and the onlooker, for example. In waking life we sometimes feel 'in two minds' about something. We think, 'Part of me wants to do this', and another part says, 'I should do that.' In dreams we can actually act out this feeling of duality.

We have seen that some characters in our dreams reflect aspects of ourselves, whereas others show us how we feel about other people. Obviously it is also possible for there to be an overlap here, just as in real life we tend to choose to relate to people who are likely to help us in some way with our personal growth. Aspects of other people that we find irritating – or aspects that we admire – are often indications of **shadow** aspects of ourselves. These are aspects that we tend to cover up or deny – more on this shortly. Choose another of your dream characters now, and then try to answer the following questions:

- Who does this character remind me of?
- Could the character also reflect an aspect of my own personality?
- What lesson is the character trying to teach me about myself?
- Does the character have a message for me about a personal relationship?

Now, bearing these questions in mind, try pretending to be your chosen character, in the same way as you did in the previous exercise.

A very good way to gain even more understanding of a dream character is to try going back into that character and actually acting out the role (see Chapter 10). This may take a bit of practice unless you are already an accomplished actor, but it can be great fun, and is well worth working with. It is especially helpful to try this in a group setting.

BECOMING EACH ASPECT OF YOUR DREAM

This exercise follows naturally from the last section, although it seems a little odd when you first try it, and some people will find it difficult. What you do is become each aspect of your dream in turn.

Mirroring yourself
The idea behind this is that not only the people, but in fact every part of your dream, can be a mirror of some aspect of yourself. The best way to explain how this works is to look at an actual example and see how it works.

JAMES GOES FLYING

*James dreams of a tiny yellow toy car that can fly through the air.
Below it, on the ground, lots of huge diggers are tearing up the
earth. The toy car is the only possible means of escape from the
diggers. It narrowly misses their clashing jaws and flies up through
the clouds towards the sun.*

*James's immediate reaction is that the diggers represent the
destruction of the earth. He feels great concern about the state
of the environment and has recently joined Friends of the Earth.
James tries going into the dream and becoming each aspect of it
in turn:*

- *'I am a tiny yellow toy car. I am like a toy car James had when
  he was a little boy. I am the only means of escape because I can
  fly above all the destruction and get an aerial view of what is
  happening. I am yellow because yellow is associated with the
  intellect. James must think of a way to stop the diggers.'*
- *'I am a digger. I have cruel steel jaws and I am slowly tearing
  the whole world apart. There are lots of us, all over the surface
  of the earth. We are unstoppable and terrifying.'*
- *'I am the sun. I am bright and give a message of hope. I warm
  and nourish the earth. If you can break through the clouds I am
  still here to help you.'*
- *'I am clouds. I obscure your view. You must rise above me in
  order to find a solution to your problem.'*

*James thinks about his digger dream for a few days and he begins to
realise that the diggers are in fact an aspect of himself, as well as an
external symbol. They represent his fear about global destruction,
and he begins to understand that he is just as responsible for it as
anybody else. As a result of the dream, James resolves to do more
to try to clean up his environment. He begins to take newspapers,
cans and bottles for recycling, and also to cycle to work whenever
possible.*

Try this method for yourself, using one of your own dreams. It is
very powerful and will give you a lot more insight into your dream

messages. Very often a symbol which has seemed obscure in its meaning will become clearer when you work with your dream in this way.

WORKING WITH EMOTIONS IN DREAMS

Meeting the shadow

The shadow is the part of the psyche that is hidden from us, where we store all the feelings and ideas that we don't really want to look at. Dream messages that have an emotional content are often telling us that it is time to have a look at that stuff. The shadow may actually appear in human form in our dreams – often as a stranger, for example, or as a person like ourselves but perhaps with different coloured hair, or of the opposite sex.

JAMES MEETS HIS SHADOW SELF

James dreams that he is having a conversation with himself. The other self is standing on top of a little hill. The other self has dark hair, whereas James has light brown hair. James is about to go to a party with a group of friends, and is trying to persuade the other self to come too. The other self is being stuffy and pompous, and refusing to come down. After a while James gets bored and wanders off.

It is easy enough to see that James is talking to a part of himself that he would rather not admit to having. That part is pedantic and boring and doesn't have much fun in life.

Finding out what we really feel

Some dreams have quite a high emotional content and leave us feeling angry, guilty, afraid, sad or happy. The emotions that we experience in our dreams are not heavily guarded, as our emotions tend to be in waking life. This is why it can be so useful to examine dream feelings – because they are likely to give us an insight into how we really feel about other people and incidents in our lives. When we can be honest about our feelings, we can begin to break free of the bonds which normally hold us back. Such bonds are often formed through childhood conditioning and from fear left over from previous life experiences. They tend to clutter us up with a lot of heavy baggage.

Feeling guilty

Have another look at Jo's marshmallow dream in Chapter 2. Here you will remember that Jo casts herself as the bad guy in the dream. She feels guilty about sneaking outside to eat some marshmallows. If a bad character appears in your dream, who makes you feel guilty, then imagine that you go back into the dream and talk to them. What would you like to say to them? Jo tries talking to her dream self in this way:

Jo	Why do you feel guilty about going out to eat the marshmallows?
Dream Jo	I ought to stay in and look after the children. Anyway, it's their marshmallow-making stuff.
Jo	Why should you look after them all the time?
Dream Jo	I'm responsible for them. It's my job.
Jo	But you need time for yourself too. Why shouldn't you have sweet things in your life too now and again?'

As a result of this conversation, Jo decided to go into town the next day with a female friend and treat them both to coffee and a cake. She felt a bit guilty for a while, but then she began to realise that she deserved it and really enjoyed herself.

If a dream makes you feel guilty it is quite likely that you are masking some hidden anger. There tends to be a veiled feeling of, 'I want to do this, only you won't let me.' Find out *who* won't let you, and why they won't. In Jo's case it was really herself!

Feeling sad

Sometimes a dream can make us feel so sad that we even wake up in tears. This can actually be very cathartic – it often means that you are groping towards deeply suppressed feelings that you have been afraid to express. Again, have a good look at other characters involved in this dream. They are usually the keys to what is going on deep down.

Feeling angry

Most of us have at some time had the experience of a jaw-clenching, tooth-grinding dream where we wake up tense and furiously angry. Find out who or what is making you feel this way, and talk it through or sort it out if you can. Blocked in anger, like any suppressed emotion, can be very bad for you.

Sarah has a dream like this, where she dreams that a bag of rice is jumping about all over her kitchen and laughing at her. She feels very angry towards it. When she writes down this dream, the rice makes her think of marriage, because you throw rice at newly-weds. She then begins to realise that she is feeling angry and trapped in her marriage, but has not wanted to admit this, for fear of rocking the boat.

EXPLORING DREAM HOUSES

Houses in dreams are often important mirrors of the way in which we see ourselves. They represent the psychic space that we live in – our own inner world. If you dream about a house, write down a detailed description of it. It doesn't matter if you feel that you are 'making up' some of your description – it will still come from your unconscious anyway.

Describing your house

♦ What type of house is it? (What sort of person do you see yourself as?)
♦ Is it big or small? (How do you feel in relation to other people?)
♦ Is your house cosy or chilly? Do you feel at home in it, or is it forbidding and unwelcoming? (Do you feel that you get on well with others, or do you see yourself as rather reserved?)
♦ Is the house old and rambling, or modern and compact? (Are you chic, or do you feel better in tatty old clothes? How modern is your outlook?)
♦ Is it clean and tidy or is it chaotic or dirty? (What is your self-image like?)

Fig 7   A dream house

◆ Does your house have any structural problems? (This can be an indication of an unconscious health warning, or an emotional problem.)

◆ Is the house well lit, or dim and dark? (This may reflect your mood state – the house may be dim and dark if you feel depressed and well lit if you are cheerful.)

All these questions can give you surprising insights into the way that you view yourself at the moment:

◆ Perhaps the roof has blown off your house – are you feeling insecure and vulnerable at present?

◆ Or perhaps water is slowly rising up to flood your cellar – do you have deeply suppressed feelings that are threatening to engulf you?

◆ Perhaps your house is cosy and welcoming – you probably feel secure and happy.

◆ Or perhaps it is too much that way, so that it is always full of other people? – Try to draw in your boundaries a bit and find more time for yourself.

Entering your house
Now let's have a look at different parts of your house and see what they can tell you about yourself.

The cellar
This may represent the darker parts of the psyche – the unconscious mind and the shadow self. Maybe you have something nasty and rotting down there – you need to get rid of that for a start! Or perhaps your cellar is full of vintage wine – have you been over indulging lately? Have a look at what is down there. You will probably find that you have a pretty good idea what it means.

The attic
This may represent the mind and the higher, spiritual aspects of the psyche. Is yours full of clutter? Then it could be time for a good spring-cleaning session. Get rid of outmoded ways of thinking that are no longer useful to you.

The door

The door corresponds to your defence against the outside world. Is yours heavy and wooden, or is it partly made of glass? If it is all glass then you may feel rather vulnerable and transparent. On the other hand, if it is too solid, then it might put other people off altogether. Does your door fulfil its purpose and protect your house, or can anybody just walk on in?

The stairs

These might show you the way up to your higher, spiritual self. Are they safe or slippery? Can you get up them easily or is there a problem of some sort?

The rooms

These represent your everyday environment. Are they light and airy, or poky and dark? Do you feel happy in your house? How could you improve your house so that you feel more at home? Can you see ways of making some of these changes in your waking life?

The garden and/or surroundings

Look outside your house too, because this relates to how you perceive your everyday environment. Does your house have a garden that you can relax in and unwind? If so, is there a fence around it or a hedge perhaps? Is your garden full of weeds, so that it makes you feel guilty? Or is it overly neat and orderly? If you are happy in your environment then you will probably feel at home in your dream garden and you will find it full of beautiful flowers, interesting nooks and crannies and secret hideaways. If you are really lucky, there might even be a gardener!

Maybe there is no garden. In this case, look at the surrounding area and see what it is like. Is there a busy, dangerous road, for example? Or a poky little yard full of rubbish? Is your house perched on a cliff near the sea? See how you can relate the surroundings of your dream house to how you feel about your life right now.

DREAMING OF WATER

If you dream about water, it may reflect your emotional state at the moment. So, for example, if you dream about a huge, calm lake, then your emotions are probably calm – you are going through a peaceful phase. Write down a detailed description of any water that you dream about. Then consider the following points and see how they could apply to your emotional frame of mind as well as to your dream water:

♦ What type of water is it – is it the sea, or a lake, pond, puddle, fountain, spring or flood?
♦ Is your water calm or rough?
♦ Is it deep or shallow?
♦ Is the water fast-flowing or sluggish?
♦ Is it clear and sparkling or murky, even polluted?
♦ What colour is the water?
♦ Is it dammed up in any way?
♦ Is the water cold or warm? Do you feel tempted to swim in it, or do you in fact fall in by mistake?

Use these clues in the same way as you did for the house exercise, in order to build up a picture of your current emotional state. Remember that it does not matter if you 'invent' some of your ideas. The more creative you are the better. If you haven't had a water dream recently, then try relaxing somewhere comfortable and then just visualising yourself as some kind of water. Then use the clues in your vision in the same way as if they were part of a dream, in order to get fresh insights about yourself.

TRAVELLING IN DREAMS

Travelling and transport in dreams often represent the way we view our way forward in life. Remember how James dreamed that his car would not start? What do you feel that this could mean?

Looking at types of transport

♦ *Cars* often represent the self, or the physical body. What sort of car is your dream car? Is it a kind that you would choose to have in real life? Is it reliable or is there something wrong with it?

♦ *Bicycles* can be a lot slower to get about on, and may be hard work, especially if the terrain is muddy or uneven. Perhaps your life is somewhat problematical at the moment? On the other hand, riding a bike might show a keen interest in green issues! If your bike ride is refreshing and exhilarating, you are probably feeling good about life in general and full of energy.

♦ *Horses* are rather variable. They can be slow and plodding, or they can be fast, exhilarating, powerful animals. A lot depends on the type of horse you encounter in your dream and, indeed, whether you actually like horses or not. This sort of difference underlines the pitfalls of having fixed meanings for dream symbols.

♦ *Travelling on foot* can be slow, but it is a good way of making sure that you have a good look at the terrain and that you don't miss things. It is also a very good way of getting in touch with nature, and keeping fit.

♦ *Flying* gives you a very good overview of your situation. Flying dreams are important enough to warrant a special section of their own later in the book.

Exploring the terrain

The terrain you travel over may represent the way you view your life's path ahead of you.

♦ *Hills* get you to a higher place, where you can get a good view, once you manage to get up them. They may represent tough obstacles, which are difficult to navigate. If you get up them easily then you are probably confident about tackling obstacles.

♦ *Barriers* such as gates or fences usually block your way forward. Can you find a way past your barrier?

♦ *Mud or swamps* are similar to water, in that they often represent emotional problems. They tend to be cloying or suffocating and hold you back. They can also make you filthy, so consider whether you have had an experience that has made you feel in some way polluted or violated.

♦ ***Ravines, cliffs or drops*** might make you feel insecure, afraid that you will fall down them and even be killed. You are probably feeling very uncertain about your future at the moment. Try to look for a safe bridge to cross over, or a way to get back 'down to earth'.

♦ ***Crossroads*** tend to appear when you have an important decision to make.

We often dream about travel or transport when we are unconsciously looking for a change in our lives. Often we are uncertain as to the right path to take, or the means of getting to where we want to be. Use your dream messages to help you to make the decisions and get you out of a stagnant situation.

QUESTIONS AND ANSWERS

I find it difficult to imagine myself as an inanimate object, such as a kettle or a table. How can I get better at doing this?
It will get easier with practice. The secret is to lighten up and not take the exercise too seriously. Try reading some children's books and poems.

What if I find one of my dream characters or objects frightening? Should I still try to act out the role?
There are no rules – don't do it if it feels too scary. But remember that it can be valuable to have a good look at the negative things as well as the positive. If a dream is really disturbing you, ask for professional guidance.

Can I use symbols that crop up in real life in the same way as dream symbols?
Yes. The more you work with dream symbols, the more you will become aware of symbolic, meaningful events in your waking life.

CHECKLIST

- ◆ Remember to explore the ways in which different aspects of your dreams mirror parts of yourself.
- ◆ Be aware of emotional issues that surface as a result of looking at your dreams.
- ◆ Have a really good look round your dream house if one appears. If not, you could try visualising one and explore that instead.
- ◆ If you are having travel or transport dreams, think about how you are 'moving' in your life. Perhaps you feel stuck, and ready for a change of some sort?
- ◆ Do you agree with the theorists who say that all the characters in our dreams are aspects of ourselves? You could discuss this question with your dream group.
- ◆ Discuss among a group of friends what type of house each person could be. Write down your ideas first and then compare notes. Do people see you as the type of house that you would expect?
- ◆ Try visualising yourself as a body of water. Go through the list of points for water dreams. What changes would you like to make in your life as a result of what you see?

Using your dream for healing 6

LOOKING AT BODY SYMBOLS

People often unconsciously use body symbols to express how they feel about something. Think of common phrases such as 'his heart was broken', 'you make me sick', or 'he's a complete airhead'. Each part of the body tends to have its own associated ideas and emotions.

When specific body parts seem important in a dream they are often being used symbolically in this way. Your dream may be expressing a particular emotion – for example, we tend to link love with the heart, and anger with a clenched fist. Alternatively, the dream may be expressing an idea – for example, the feet are for going forward in life, and the stomach could be for 'digesting' ideas.

Have a look at Figure 8, which suggests some of the common ideas associated with different parts of the body. Obviously this is only a short list and you can begin to add your own ideas. Begin to listen when people are speaking and hear how often they mention body symbols. Our body is a very important part of our life, and it is not surprising that this type of symbolism is so common. Look through your dream journal and see if you can pick out any body symbols. Here are a few common examples.

Finding your teeth falling out

This is a surprisingly common dream. It is sometimes just a natural anxiety – perhaps you need to go to the dentist! But teeth are for biting, so the dream may be about hidden anger. Or perhaps you

Body part	Common associations	Examples of related phrases
Head	Thinking, intellect.	Using your head. Airhead. Egghead. Keeping your head.
Heart	Love, emotions, compassion.	Broken heart. Heart of gold.
Arms/hands	Holding, grasping, carrying.	Having your hands full. Long arm of the law.
Legs/feet	Moving forward, staying grounded.	Feet firmly on the ground. Putting your best foot forward.
Tongue	Speech, gossip.	Sharp tongue. Evil tongue. Holding your tongue.
Eyes	Seeing the way forward, seeing things clearly.	Having your eyes opened. Sharp-eyed.
Ears	Hearing, listening.	A sympathetic ear. Walls have ears. Being all ears.
Nose	Being astute, or nosy.	Nosy Parker. Having a nose for something.
Stomach	Digesting and assimilating.	No stomach for it. It makes me sick.
Lungs	Taking in energy or life.	Needing breathing space. Taking a deep breath.
Spine/neck	Support, flexibility, moral strength.	Pain in the neck. No backbone. Stiff-necked.
Mouth	Eating and communication.	Big mouth. Stiff upper lip. Tight-lipped.
Fingers/ thumb	Picking up details, gesturing. Ring finger – marriage. Index finger – pointing.	Pointing the finger. Putting two fingers up. Thumbs up/down. More sense in my little finger.
Shoulders	Carrying burdens and responsibilities.	Shouldering a burden. Having broad shoulders. Giving the cold shoulder.
Throat	Swallowing and speech.	It sticks in my throat. Swallowing a tall story.
Knees	Awe, fear, strong emotions, humility.	On bended knee. Going weak at the knees.
Genitals	Sexuality, power, creative force. Taboos.	Dickhead. Being a prick. Vagina dentata (look it up!).
Skin	Protection.	Thin-skinned. Thick-skinned.
Teeth	Biting and chewing.	Biting off more than you can chew.

Fig 8   Commonly occurring body symbols

feel that you have bitten off more than you can chew. Our teeth actually do fall out when we make the transition from child to adult, and again from maturity to old age. This dream therefore commonly occurs when you are at a transition point in your life.

Losing your hair

This is also common in dreams. It may mean that you are anxious about your health, or about ageing. If your hair changes colour in the dream, then you may be exploring new aspects of your personality. Our hair is a very important part of our appearance, so you may be exploring aspects of how you relate to others. Take note of the new hair colour and consider what it might mean.

Needing the toilet

This often occurs in dreams as a gentle reminder that we had better wake up and go. If you dream this dream and find that you do not really need to go, then it is more likely that the dream is about an issue that you need to deal with, or release from your life. This is particularly likely if the toilet is dirty, or inaccessible or disturbing in some way. Toilet dreams also tend to occur when you are getting ready to start something new in life or to go on a journey – whether actual or metaphorical. After all, people often pay a visit before setting off somewhere, going into a meeting, sitting down for a meal, etc.

BEING YOUR OWN DREAM DOCTOR

Sometimes people have a striking dream, or even a recurring dream, about a particular area of the body. Studies have shown that this can occasionally be an unconscious health warning, so it may be worth taking note of. The message may be a simple one, telling you to cut down on junk food, or stop smoking. However, if the apparent message worries you, then it could be a good idea to talk to your doctor. It does no harm to have a check-up, and your dream just might be a valuable early warning signal.

Remember that cars and houses sometimes represent the physical body, so if your car refuses to start, or your drains are blocked, then this could be a health worry dream. Of course, it would be wrong to imagine that you can diagnose your own illness or treat it in some way. It is more a question of being aware of possible cues to slow down, rest more, eat less and so on. Dreams to watch for are:

- ♦ problems with your car
- ♦ problems with a house
- ♦ dreams involving violence or pain, for example, being stabbed in the chest
- ♦ loss of hair or teeth
- ♦ dreams of premature ageing

Any of these dreams could carry a health warning, or they might be related to your emotional state. However, as mind and body are so closely linked, it is worthwhile to be aware of both aspects. A prolonged period of stress of any kind is often followed by illness in the body.

EATING FOOD IN DREAMS

Eating is one of our most regular waking activities, and also one of the most pleasurable ones. However, nowadays food is often also connected with guilt in a lot of people, wondering if they are eating too much food, too much fat, not enough cabbage, and so on. If you dream about food, you need to consider different approaches to your dream interpretation.

Being nourished by food

Food is nourishment first and foremost. Therefore if you dream about food there may be a message about the way you nurture yourself.

- ♦ If you are looking for food, consider what is lacking in your life. Assuming actual food is not an issue, perhaps you are short of friends, or of intellectual stimulation – 'food for thought'. Or maybe the food you seek is of a more spiritual nature. Food is an obvious symbol for life itself, so are you enjoying life at the moment?

♦ If you are over-eating in your dream, perhaps you are being over-stimulated in some way; or else a situation has become tedious and dull. Think about whether you are doing too much, or having too busy a social life. Or perhaps you are simply eating too much food in waking life and your unconscious is prompting you to cut down.

♦ If the dream food is dull, unsatisfying or unpleasant in some way, this would tend to reflect some aspect of your current life. Think about what is boring you or frustrating you.

♦ Similarly, being forced to eat food that you don't want might indicate that you are taking on board too much of other people's attitudes or 'stuff'. It might be time to break away and do some independent thinking!

Looking at the colour of your food

Food colours in dreams may be unusual, or stand out in a striking way. This often means that you need more of the type of energy related to that colour. For example, if you dream about green foods, this might be your body telling you to eat more greens or salads. On a more spiritual level, the colour green is associated with healing and love. If you have recently been through an emotional trauma, then this could be the message in your green dream. Try bringing the colour green into your life in one or more of the following ways:

♦ Eat more green foods.
♦ Light a green candle and meditate for a while by concentrating on its flame.
♦ Buy something green for your home.
♦ Soak in a green herbal bath.
♦ Buy yourself a green crystal such as aventurine or moss agate, and carry it around with you for a while.

You can easily adapt this list for other food colours that may appear in your dreams. Refer back to the list of colour associations in Figure 5 for help with this.

Savouring your dream food

The quality of the food in your dream is very important.

- ◆ *Sweet food* can mean that you are enjoying sweet things in your life. If it is sickly or cloying, however, it could represent something you have had enough of, or something or somebody artificially 'sweet'.
- ◆ *Tough food* could represent a tough situation or character.
- ◆ *Bitter food* – what do you feel bitter about?
- ◆ *Savoury or spicy food* probably means that you are feeling satisfied and excited with your life at the moment.
- ◆ *Unsatisfactory or phantom food* – are you pursuing an unsatisfactory or illusory goal?
- ◆ *Nasty or sickening food* may indicate that whatever it is that preoccupies your mind at the moment is not really good for you.

Observing your surroundings as you eat

The place where you are eating, and possibly other people who are eating with you, can give other important clues. They will usually relate to the situation that your unconscious is trying to work with.

Sarah goes to a party

Sarah dreams that she goes to a party where there is a huge buffet, but everything she tries seems tasteless and dull. She feels as if she is eating it more to be polite than anything else. Everyone else seems to be enjoying it, but she is trying to find a reason to sneak away. When Sarah writes this dream down she realises that the boring food could represent the way she feels about her life right now. It feels dull and tasteless, and she is bored by a lot of her social life. She needs to find out what energises her.

Thinking about eating food in dreams makes a useful transition between physical healing and mental or spiritual healing. Food dreams can bring a message on any or all three levels. The next two sections are about healing and balancing yourself more on the mental and spiritual levels.

WORKING WITH ANIMAL SYMBOLS

Throughout history humans have tended to regard animals as important messengers, both in waking life and in dreams. Shamans, who were the spiritual leaders in tribal society, often worked with animal symbols through trance, meditation and dreams. Each familiar animal or bird had its own associated characteristics and energies. Individual people, and sometimes whole tribes, often had a particular power animal or 'totem'. This animal was a spiritual guide, mentor and protector, or symbolised the energy of the tribe.

If an animal or bird appears in your dream, you can consider its message in several different ways:

♦ Does the animal remind you of one you have known, such as a pet or farm animal?
♦ Is it one of your favourite animals? (Children will often have a favourite animal, instinctively choosing one that will give them beneficial energies.)
♦ Does it link up with your birth sign, or another important symbol in your life, such as a business or group logo?
♦ Does it feel as if your animal is giving you a special message? If so, this could be your personal power animal.

Finding your power animal

A power animal is one that will give you energies, insights or protection that you especially need. This can be a short-term thing for a period of life when you need a particular animal. It is also possible to find an animal that is a life-long totem animal. This is an animal that feels especially important to you and will tend to appear in your dreams now and again. Such an animal can be a guide and protector, helping to balance the energies in your psyche. Having pictures or other objects associated with your special animal can be empowering.

Understanding animal energies

As with any symbol appearing in your dreams, it is important to realise that animals can carry a personal significance as well as a more widely recognised collective meaning. For example, somebody who has been bitten by a rabbit may not see the same cute cuddly animal that most of us would. Therefore some of the ideas below may not feel right for you, so go with your own instincts.

- ◆ *Bird.* Freedom. Joyful song. Messenger.
- ◆ *Cat.* Independence, female energy, mysterious, aloof, creature of the night.
- ◆ *Dog.* Loyal, trustworthy friend. Can be subservient.
- ◆ *Horse.* Swift, powerful, noble. Takes you places.
- ◆ *Pig.* Very intelligent. Signifies wealth and prosperity but can warn of over-indulgence.
- ◆ *Hen.* Fussy, mothering instinct, cosy.
- ◆ *Eagle.* High-flier, keen-eyed and far-seeing.
- ◆ *Owl.* Mysterious bird of the night. Silent, psychic and wise. Sometimes associated with death.
- ◆ *Fish.* Slippery customer, a cool water dweller. Some, for example the salmon in Celtic lore, are traditionally wise and ancient.
- ◆ *Monster.* Something that you are afraid of. You may need to confront this monster – they are often not as bad as they seem.

There are many good websites to help you understand animal messages. Try to build up personal associations of your own as well – you might like to make a special animal glossary at the back of your dream journal.

Mythical beasts

Mythical animals can also have important roles to play in our dream world. You will find many ideas about them in myths and legends, which can also be a useful source of ideas about real animals.

- ◆ The *dragon* often appears guarding a pile of treasure, or fighting with a bold knight. There are many different types of dragons, often associated with one of the four elements – earth, air, fire and water. All are larger than life, fantastic and powerful. Chinese dragons are often lucky.

♦ The *phoenix* is associated with fire and also with death and reincarnation. It may indicate a huge upsurge of new energy in your psyche.

♦ *Mermaids* and *mermen* are interesting, as they are half-human and half-fish and so can act as go-betweens between the conscious and unconscious realms. But merpeople can be dangerous if they lure you beneath the waves, away from the mortal realm.

♦ *Fairies* can also be very dangerous and you have to keep on the right side of them. They may even steal children, or human souls. On the other hand, they can guide us in the dream world and even befriend and help us.

♦ *Unicorns* are mysterious, psychic, lunar beasts. They are rare and elusive and can only be captured by maidens – in other words, those who are innocent and pure in spirit.

TALKING WITH YOUR INNER CHILD

We all have an **inner child** – that part of our psyche that has remained with us since we were children. When you feel in a light-hearted, silly or creative mood, that is when your inner child is showing itself. It may also manifest as a part of the self that feels small, defenceless or neglected.

The inner child quite often appears in our dreams and is a very important figure. If you dream about a child then consider:

♦ Is it a child you actually know, or have known?
♦ Or is it an unknown child that seems to reflect an aspect of your own psyche?

Remember that because your dreams often act like a mirror, your dream child may represent an aspect of yourself, even if it is a child whom you actually know in real life. Try to work out what it is about the child that reminds you of yourself. Sometimes it can be helpful to write out a conversation between you and your dream-child in your journal. This may help you to understand what your inner child wants.

Finding out how your inner child is feeling

Is the child in your dream happy and playful? Or is it angry or unhappy in some way? Some aspects of our emotional behaviour as adults develop in our early childhood, so it can be interesting to find out how your dream-child feels. If your child is not happy, then try to imagine that you are talking to it. Find out what it wants or needs. Is there a way in which your adult self shares this need? If so, can you think of ways of fulfilling the need? For example, perhaps your inner child is lonely – try getting out more and making new friends, perhaps joining a group of some kind.

Seeing how your inner child is dressed

Is your child well dressed and cared for, or is it ragged, dirty and unloved? If your child seems to be neglected, try to find ways of pampering yourself more. Do something that you really enjoy, or buy yourself a new outfit or a little present. Nurture your inner child by caring properly for yourself.

Watching what your inner child is doing

♦ *If your child is playing happily*, you are quite likely going through a happy, creative phase in your life.
♦ *If your child is ill or wounded*, part of you may need healing. If you cannot do this for yourself, talk to a professional carer such as a spiritual leader or a therapist.
♦ *If your child is locked up or confined*, perhaps you need more freedom to express your playful, creative side. Try to have more fun and free time.
♦ *If your child is lost*, perhaps you fear losing part of yourself. Are other people dominating your life in some way, or are you overwhelmed by a difficult situation?

When you begin to look at your inner child dream, think about these and any other points that seem relevant. If you don't dream about a child, then you could try visualising a meeting with your inner child, just as you may have done with the dream house and water exercises.

JO TALKS TO HER INNER CHILD

Jo dreams that she is at the day nursery where she works. All the children are playing happily, apart from one little girl who sits in a corner crying. Jo feels very sorry for this little girl, and asks her what is wrong.

'I'm sick of all these children. I want my mummy,' wails the child. Jo realises that she works with children all day long and then goes home to more of the same. She is totally neglecting her own inner child. All her dreams are telling her in different ways that she needs to nurture herself more. She decides to do something about this and so she enrols in a yoga class on her day off and begins to have that as a special time for herself.

QUESTIONS AND ANSWERS

Is there a way to find my power animal even if I don't dream of one?

Yes. Your power animal may appear in waking life as a real animal that you are especially drawn to. Or you may be drawn to buy a t-shirt with a tiger on, or perhaps a dolphin ornament. You can also try meeting your animal by asking it to appear in a waking visualisation. Simply relax and imagine that you are in a place that you love, such as walking through a wood or by the sea. Mentally ask your animal guide to appear and see what happens.

Can I have more than one power animal?

Yes. Sometimes we need to work with the energies of more than one animal at a time. They may even appear to be conflicting ones, such as lion and deer. Each animal represents a different aspect of the psyche.

Are there other 'inner selves', apart from the child?

We all have many different inner selves, each of which is a kind of sub-personality of its own. Our different moods and behaviours can sometimes reflect this. You might meet an inner teenager, for example, or a baby, or a person of the opposite sex. Conflicts that were unresolved at earlier stages of our lives sometimes appear in dreams of this sort. The beliefs and behaviours of people's 'sub-personalities' may conflict, which partly explains why people can be so unpredictable and contradictory.

CHECKLIST

- ◆ Be aware of body symbols in your dreams. They are important and can sometimes give a timely health warning.
- ◆ Remember that dreams about food are about nourishing yourself. This may mean literally, by altering your diet, or it may mean nourishing your mind or spirit.
- ◆ If an animal begins to appear from time to time in your dreams, it may be your power animal. Listen to the important message it has for you. There are many ways in which you can encourage your power animal energy – for example, buy yourself a garment or a piece of jewellery representing your animal, or you might prefer a picture or an ornament.
- ◆ Get to know your inner child and take time to talk to it when it appears in your dreams. Find out ways in which you can see to its wants and needs.

Creating a dream dictionary 7

TAKING THE DRIVER'S SEAT

One of the most important aspects of learning how to work with your dreams is to realise that you, and you alone, are the expert on your own dreams. You are in control, in the driver's seat. So, if you talk to somebody else about one of your dreams and they offer an explanation that does not feel quite right to you, then you don't necessarily have to take their ideas on board. In fact, sometimes talking a dream through in this way will put you in touch with your own 'gut feeling' about a dream, and so bring you closer to a true understanding.

It should be quite clear by now that dream symbols may have many meanings. There are common meanings that most people would understand – archetypal meanings that are common to all human beings – plus personal meanings that are known only to you. This chapter is about how to build up a useful dream dictionary of your own, expanding ideas about your own personal symbolism. Before you begin, bear in mind the following points:

♦ You may feel that you want to keep your dream journal, and maybe even your dictionary, totally private. You might feel more willing to share your dreams at a later date when you are more confident.

♦ Keep your dream journal near your bed so that you can reach it easily. When you have written a dream down, take time really to 'listen' to the dream and get a feel for it, before you begin to analyse it.

♦ Don't be afraid of your own unconscious mind. It belongs to you and is a part of yourself that can offer valuable insights for personal growth.

♦ Encourage your unconscious to realise that you are now interested in your dreams. You can assist the process by bringing more creative activity into your waking life as well. Try painting, music, creative writing, dance or simply being out in the fresh air more, or doing some gardening.

♦ Above all, enjoy your dreams and the journey of getting to know yourself better.

We have already looked at some common dream themes, such as the house dream, water dream and travel dream. Before starting on your dream dictionary, let's have a look at a few more.

LOOKING AT SOME COMMON DREAM THEMES

Falling

This dream can take many forms. Perhaps you fall off a cliff, or down a deep, dark hole. Theories abound as to the cause of falling dreams. They are sometimes attributed to physical causes such as the simple muscle relaxation effect as you fall asleep, or even to bouts of indigestion! Symbolically, however, falling tends to feel dangerous, and it could indicate that you feel out of control in some way. The context of the fall will give you more clues.

♦ *Falling off a cliff* often means that you are feeling very vulnerable, and unsure of the ground you are standing on.

♦ *Falling into a deep, dark hole* is often connected with a fear of exploring unconscious ideas.

♦ *Falling off a ladder* – think about whether you were climbing up or down. Climbing up tends to indicate working towards a personal goal. Climbing down could mean coming down from a place where you felt unsafe, or it could be to do with climbing down into the depths of your unconscious.

Falling dreams often occur when you are going through a rapid stage of personal growth.

Flying

This is another common dream theme. You may find yourself flying high above the ground, enjoying a bird's-eye view, or you may find that you can barely get off the ground. Flying dreams are often related to ambitions in life, so if you are soaring high then you are probably doing well. If, on the other hand, it is hard work and you find lots of obstacles in your way, then perhaps it is time to reassess where you are going.

Another popular explanation for flying dreams is that they occur when the spirit enters the non physical **astral body** and flies free. Obviously this interpretation depends on your personal beliefs. It is certainly true that flying dreams are often associated with a sensation of great exhilaration and freedom.

Being watched

This dream can take many forms. You are sitting on the toilet and suddenly realise a crowd of people is staring at you. Or you find yourself stark naked in the middle of the supermarket. Such dreams usually involve embarrassment in one form or another. They may indicate that you are feeling vulnerable or exposed in some way, and perhaps under attack from others. You might even have a secret that makes you feel guilty about something.

Wearing unusual clothing

Clothing tends to represent the attitudes and personality that we show to other people. If you are wearing ordinary comfortable clothes in your dream, then you are probably fairly comfortable with your current image. If, however, your clothes seem tight it could indicate that you have 'outgrown' some of your attitudes or roles, and need to 'change' them. If your clothes seem ridiculous, perhaps you are afraid of being laughed at, or maybe you just want to lighten up a bit and play the clown.

Sometimes you may find that you are dressed in the clothes of a particular character – I once dreamed that I was dressed as Dennis the Menace, a cartoon character from my childhood. If this happens in your dream, try to assess which aspects of that character you find empowering or threatening. (For example, Dennis the Menace was telling me that I needed to be more carefree and childish, even 'naughty'.)

Being delayed or late

This common type of dream has already been mentioned in James's case study. Everything goes wrong, you are late for an important appointment, or you miss the bus. Do you worry about being late in your waking life? Or do you feel that you are always in a rush, trying to fit too many things into your day? Perhaps you actually feel out of control of your life. If you feel that any of these things could be true, you may need to relax more and 'chill out'. Try to spend time simply being, as well as doing.

Being paralysed

Perhaps you get stuck in a dream lift, or simply fall over and find that you cannot move. My mother had a recurring dream of this kind as a young adult and then she had polio and her dream became a nightmarish reality – so for her it was a predictive dream. This kind of dream often occurs at times when we feel that life is frustrating. We feel unable, or unwilling, to make a necessary change. We might even feel 'paralysed' by fear. Is there a change that you know needs to happen in your life?

Some researchers have more physical explanations for the sensation of paralysis during sleep. During REM sleep, for example, the muscles are virtually paralysed. In the past, sleep paralysis was sometimes known as being 'hag-ridden' or having a 'hag-attack', because it was believed that witches could attack people in their sleep and paralyse them.

DISCOVERING YOUR OWN SYMBOLS

By now you will probably be building up some ideas about dream symbols that have personal meanings for you. For example, perhaps you tend to associate bread with your mother, because she baked all the family's bread when you were a child. The more that you work with symbols, both in dreams and in waking life, the more insights you will gain.

Playing the symbol game

This game can be played on your own or with friends. It will help you to think in more intuitive ways about symbols and their meanings. Look around and choose any object you see, just as you would for a game of 'I-spy'. Supposing you choose the sun, for example:

- *What ideas do you immediately associate with your object? Be imaginative and think of as many ideas as you can.*
  Warmth, growth, holidays, sunburn, deserts . . .
- *What feelings do you associate with your object?*
  Happy, relaxed, lazy, hot . . .
- *Can you think of any stories, songs, films, etc. connected with your object?*
  'The sun has got his hat on'
  The sun god Apollo in Greek myths.
- *Do you have any interesting memories connected with your object?*
  Seeing the sun in partial eclipse when I was at school.
- *Try to describe your object to someone who doesn't know what it is.*
  It is our nearest star. It is very hot and warms the earth. It is bright, round and yellow . . .

This game can lead you to all kinds of associations that you may not otherwise have thought of. It is very interesting to compare different people's ideas.

Looking for symbols in everyday life

Remember to keep an eye out for events and objects that could be symbolic in some way. For example, we have all probably had the experience of a certain number which seems to crop up over and over again. It appears as a house number, a birthday, a lottery number and so on. Or perhaps your washing machine floods the kitchen – have you been feeling more emotional than usual? Looking for symbols in this way can be fascinating and sometimes highly amusing as well. It will certainly help you to understand dream symbols more readily.

MAKING YOUR DREAM DICTIONARY

You could begin your dream dictionary in the back of your dream journal, but it will probably get quite long after a while, so it is better to use a special notebook or file. The best thing to use is something that has an A-to-Z indexing system. An address book is one possibility, but even better would be a file with A-to-Z file dividers. That way you can add in more sheets of paper wherever you need them.

Divide each page up as shown in the example in Figure 9. The page shows an extract from James's dream dictionary. Some of the symbols he has chosen have already cropped up in his dreams, whereas others have been included simply out of interest. His dictionary will build up gradually as he progresses.

If you look at the entry under 'clothes', you will see that James has not yet put in any personal associations. Sometimes you will not think of any at first, so just go along with the common meanings until you find ideas that feel right for you. Use various sources to help you with ideas. Just to remind you of a few, you could use:

♦ a dictionary
♦ a dream dictionary
♦ myths and stories
♦ free association

Looking again at James's sample page, you will see that some of his own associations are very personal. For example, look at the entry under 'crossroads'. James has a particular association here with a local ghost, which means that crossroads could appear as being rather scary in his dreams! It is this kind of thing that makes your personal dream dictionary both useful and interesting.

Symbol	Common meaning	Own meaning	Appearance in dream
Cabbage	Healthy green food. Dull person.	Yuk. I hate it. School dinners.	
Cactus	Prickly person or difficult situation.	Auntie Mary's kitchen, because she has them on the windowsill.	
Cage	Fear, feeling trapped.	Hamsters – childhood.	
Clothes	Public image.		17 March, dream about being unable to find clean shirt for interview.
Computer	Logical thinking.	My work, creative ways of thinking.	11 April, dream about small boy playing on the computer.
Crossroads	Choice to be made. Unsure which way to go.	Ghost at crossroads near my house.	
Crowd	Strangers, anonymity.	Feeling alone in centre of London.	
Deer		Walking in the forest.	
Diving bell	Ability to go underwater, breathe underwater.	Exploring emotions. Exploring new environment.	14 March, dream about murky pond.
Driving	Getting places. Status symbol (cars).	Appears a lot in frustrating dreams – car won't start, I get lost, etc.	Common theme.

Fig 9   A sample page from James's dream dictionary

FINDING SPECIAL SYMBOLS

Occasionally a symbol that seems to be particularly important may crop up in a dream. Sometimes this special symbol recurs in different dreams, or it may come up only once but you just know that it feels important to you.

Special symbols may be well-known ones that are found in myths and stories. They also appear as birth signs, business logos, religious symbols and so on. Or your symbol might be important to you alone. Either way, finding a special symbol in a dream can be very empowering and you should take special note when one occurs.

The special symbol may represent an aspect of your belief system or culture. More personal special symbols tend to represent an aspect of your own psyche. Look out for the following:

+ *Religious symbols* – for example, the Christian cross.
+ *National symbols* – for instance, the Welsh dragon.
+ *Lucky symbols* – such as a four-leafed clover.
+ *Mythical symbols* – like the Holy Grail in Arthurian legends.
+ *Personal symbols* – such as an owl brooch you have had since childhood.

If a special symbol does appear in your dreams, take time to decide what the symbol means to you. How did you feel when you had the dream about the symbol? It can be very satisfying to work with special symbols in your waking life as well. Try any of the following ideas:

+ Draw or paint your symbol and then put the artwork somewhere you will see it often, such as by your bed or in the kitchen.
+ You might be lucky enough to find your symbol represented in an item of jewellery. Wearing your special symbol reminds you constantly of its meaning for you.
+ See if you can find simple objects that represent your symbol. For example, you might find it on a mug or a tea towel.

♦ You might be able to adapt the symbol for your personal use – for example, as a business logo or as a letter heading.

JAMES BUYS A SUN SIGN

James has a strange dream about a big yellow sun sign. It has a smiling face and makes him feel happy and full of energy. When he wakes up he feels that the sun sign is giving him a special message that he is going to have a really good day. He goes shopping later that morning and to his surprise he sees a similar sun sign in a shop window. He buys the sun sign and takes it home to hang in his living room. He finds that it gives him a very positive energy and begins to wonder if he could use it in a business logo.

QUESTIONS AND ANSWERS

What does it mean if I dream I am being chased?
This is a common anxiety dream which can be very frightening. Take a good look at who or what is chasing you. It is quite likely to be related in some way to an issue that you are avoiding and that your unconscious is trying to draw your attention to! It is sometimes useful to 're-enter' the dream and confront your pursuer. You can learn more about this technique in Chapter 9.

What if I dream about the past?
How does the situation you dream of relate to your life in the present? If you are back at school in your dream then maybe you are once more in a learning situation. If you have been bereaved and dream that you are back with the person you loved, then this may be part of the healing and grieving process. Dreaming of the past may also be pointing out unresolved issues that are still lurking in your psyche.

What if I have a recurring dream?
This kind of dream is particularly interesting. It may indicate a deep-seated issue that you are not addressing. Your unconscious is trying to get through to you, so pay attention! Intriguingly, recurring dreams can sometimes predict the future, like my mother's paralysis

dream. You can read more about predictive dreams and recurring dreams in the next chapter.

CHECKLIST

♦ Ask among your friends to find out which of them has ever had a flying dream. What do people tend to think this dream means? Why do you think it is such a common theme?

♦ If you were to choose a special symbol for yourself, what would that symbol be?

♦ Always remember that you are the expert on your own dreams. Discuss them with others, but don't worry if their interpretations are different from your own.

♦ Look out for common themes occurring in your dreams. What issues might they be pointing to?

♦ Begin to create your own dream dictionary.

♦ Be aware of special symbols in your dreams and try to use them in your waking life, like James did with his sun sign.

Exploring some common dream types

8

FACING NIGHTMARES

Most people will experience nightmares from time to time during their lives. A nightmare is a dream that leaves us with feelings of great anxiety, guilt, fear or even terror. They are quite common and some people have them frequently. The unpleasant emotions are often accompanied by physical symptoms – the person may wake up breathing hard, heart pounding, perhaps crying. Sometimes people will scream and wake others in the house.

Looking at the causes of nightmares

♦ Nightmares are sometimes caused by eating a large or rich meal shortly before sleeping. It is possible that the biochemical process of digesting the meal may interfere with normal sleep patterns.

♦ Withdrawal from alcohol or from other drugs such as some types of sleeping pills may be accompanied by nightmares.

♦ Illness may also cause nightmares, especially if you are running a high temperature.

♦ Undergoing an upsetting experience during the day or watching a disturbing film may cause nightmares.

♦ Paralysis nightmares, during which the victim feels unable to move, even if attempting to flee from danger, may be linked to the REM phase of sleep, when the muscles are deeply relaxed.

♦ If you are going through a difficult phase emotionally, then it is more likely that you will experience nightmares. Worry and anxiety can interfere with sleep patterns, causing disjointed sleep, insomnia and nightmares.

♦ Nightmares may also relate to traumatic experiences in your past.

Common types of nightmare

♦ Being pursued by something or somebody threatening.
♦ Feeling paralysed, unable to move or to escape.
♦ Exams, tests or interviews that go horribly wrong, or which you are totally incapable of coping with.
♦ Trying to get somewhere on time and being endlessly delayed and frustrated.
♦ Being strangled or suffocated.
♦ Experiencing or witnessing violence.
♦ Losing control, for example falling, driving a car that is out of control, riding a bolting horse, wetting oneself in public, etc.

Nightmares are very personal experiences and you may well find that your own nightmare does not fit into any of these types. Sometimes the nightmare can be about something that nobody else would find disturbing at all. The important thing is to acknowledge that you find your experience disturbing and then try to deal with it.

Dealing with your nightmare

♦ First of all, try to pinpoint what exactly it is that disturbs you in your nightmare. For example, if there is a scary monster in your dream, ask yourself what it is about the monster that really scares you. Is it the eyes perhaps, or its enormous size? Looking at your monster clinically in this way will begin to make it less frightening, even faintly ridiculous.

♦ Both modern therapists and more traditional dream workers tend to agree that a good way to deal with a nightmare is sometimes to face it head-on. If you start to have a recurring nightmare, then try to remind yourself before you sleep that this time you will face your problem. You may then find yourself equipped with a weapon such as a sword next time your monster appears, or you may suddenly find a way out of your nightmare dilemma that you had not thought of before.

♦ You may find that you can talk to an attacker, if not during the nightmare itself, then perhaps afterwards in a visualisation exercise. Try asking questions such as 'Who are you?', 'What do you want?' or 'What part of me do you represent?' Write down any answers you get, even if they seem irrelevant at the time.

♦ Draw your nightmare. This is a very helpful method to use with children. They are good at inventing cages to confine their monster, or hoovering it up with a special vacuum cleaner.

♦ Talk about your nightmare with someone else. Try to find out what emotional experience it relates to.

♦ Appoint yourself a guardian. You could try taking a special crystal to bed, for example, that will protect you as you sleep. Children are often comforted by being told about their own special guardian angel.

♦ Remember to consider physical causes too, such as eating too late, or drug effects.

SARAH MEETS A TALL FLOBBERY MONSTER

Sarah is walking alone down a dark lane in her dream, when to her horror she sees a 'tall flobbery monster' blocking her path. She becomes semi-lucid at this point (see later in this chapter), and remembers that it is a good idea to confront her monster. To her surprise she discovers that the monster is friendly and he is sick of people running away from him. He is very lonely, and glad to talk to Sarah.

FINDING THE SECRET OF THE UNIVERSE – VISIONARY DREAMS

From time to time you may have a dream that feels especially important in some way. You may even feel, on awakening, that you have mastered the secret of the universe or the meaning of life! Such dreams sometimes prove disappointing on reflection, after you have written them down. What seemed like profound wisdom may turn out to be trite, enigmatic or even ridiculous.

Fig 10   Scary monsters

However, many people do recall dreams that they feel have really changed the course of their lives. The dream may bring new understanding or help during a critical period of development. Such dreams are often recalled as rather mystical experiences and the dreamer may feel that the message has come from God, or from some other higher power outside the self. Jung called these visionary dreams 'big dreams', and art and literature are full of them.

Receiving help or insight
A visionary dream may help us in different ways:

♦ It may lead to a new invention. Elias Howe (1819–67), who patented the first proper lockstitch sewing machine, claimed to have been guided by a visionary dream that gave him the idea of putting the hole at the tip of the needle.
♦ It may help us to figure out a problem. A famous example is research chemist Friedrich August Kekulé (1829–96), who had a vision about a snake swallowing its own tail while he was trying to understand the structure of the benzene molecule. Benzene consists of six carbon atoms and six hydrogen atoms that link together in the form of a ring.
♦ A visionary dream sometimes contains a warning or advice, either for you or another person. For example, Joseph's dream in the Bible, during which an angel appeared and warned him to take his family away to safety in Egypt.
♦ On a more personal level, the visionary dream may offer profound insight into the deeper meaning and purpose of your life.

Characteristically the visionary dream seems to extend beyond the normal experience of the dreamer. Sometimes they may occur because our unconscious mind is busy working away on a problem while we sleep. At other times it really does feel as if we are receiving some sort of external guidance. In either event, visionary dreams are often important and one should pay them special attention. Warning dreams in particular should be listened to.

TAKING HEED OF DREAM WARNINGS

Warnings in dreams are quite common and vary from everyday 'reminder' dreams to more important warnings such as the health warnings discussed earlier.

Reminding yourself in dreams

Reminder dreams are small warning dreams that occur when our unconscious is prompting us to get on with everyday tasks that we have put off. For example, you might dream about a cross man in an office labelled Inland Revenue. Have you forgotten to fill in your tax return form? Dream messages of this sort can be useful in drawing our attention to things that we know deep down ought to be done.

Everyday warnings

Perhaps you dream that your washing machine floods the kitchen, only to find that it happens in reality the next day. This is probably because you have picked up on subtle cues such as the washing machine making a slightly unusual noise. This type of DIY dream often connects up with messages about the self as well as our home environment. The washing machine dream is connected with water – and, strangely enough, it may occur at a time when you are feeling extra emotional, tearful and upset. So, if your household appliances begin to play up – either in your dreams or in real life – have a look for symbolic messages of this kind. Ask yourself:

♦ What does my dream symbol represent? For example, supposing you dream that your drains are blocked. Drains are for getting rid of unwanted stuff, especially of the liquid variety. The dream may be drawing your attention to a physical problem, such as constipation. Alternatively you may be holding on to emotional baggage that you would be better off without.

♦ What can I do to follow up the warning? Looking at the drain example, perhaps you could try to eat more roughage or drink plenty of water. Or if you feel that it relates more to your emotional self then try to find an outlet for your blocked-up feelings. Talk to somebody, or work your feelings off in physical activity or in creative ways.

Disaster warnings

Occasionally people have a dream that seems to be a clear warning about a disaster such as an accident while travelling. If you do have a dream of this kind that really disturbs you, then it is probably as well to cancel your trip. Even if no disaster subsequently happens, you will save yourself a good deal of anxiety about the trip. Try to think about what aspect of your journey is frightening you. Sometimes disaster dreams are actually warnings that something is wrong with our health or with an important relationship.

Warnings about others

Sometimes our dreams will give us subtle hints that all is not well in a personal relationship. Maybe on the surface everything appears to be fine, but the dream message from our unconscious tells us that deep down we are not being fooled. For example, you might dream about fire breaking out in a cupboard inside your dream house. This dream might suggest that you are hiding away angry feelings. If you go on suppressing them they may eventually do considerable damage. If you have a dream of this sort that you feel could be to do with a relationship, then try not to ignore it – try to work out what the message is about and then talk it through with the person concerned.

Sometimes we dream that harm of some kind comes to one of our loved ones. Dreams of this sort are common, so don't panic! First of all, consider whether the dream could actually be a warning about a problem such as a health issue. If not, think about whether the person's problem is actually mirroring part of your own psyche. For example, you might dream about a lost child. This dream could really be about some aspect of your own inner child that you lost while you were growing up.

Exploring warning dreams

If you have a warning dream, you might like to explore some of the following questions:

♦ Is there some aspect of my life that I need to sort out?

♦ Have I been putting off something that I know needs to be done, such as going for a health check or getting the gutters mucked out?

♦ Am I suppressing looking more deeply at some aspect of a relationship, perhaps in order to keep things peaceful?

NOTING COINCIDENCES IN DREAMS

Coincidences make a fascinating study, both in dream work and in waking life. If you study your dreams regularly, you may find dream themes that coincidentally link up with events in waking life. One of my favourite coincidences is a really insane one: after a huge personal crisis I dreamed of a toilet which exploded in my bathroom, sending horrible, smelly mess everywhere. Believe it or not, a day or two later somebody told me about a friend of his who had put some chemicals down the toilet, followed by a fag end. Guess what happened . . . ?

Coincidences of this sort in our dream world are mysterious, and much more common than you would think. Once you begin to record your dreams you may well find examples of your own. You might find it interesting to keep a special coincidence journal, collecting instances from both waking and dreaming experiences. If you do this, try to set a few ground rules as to what you count as a coincidence. For example:

♦ Set a deadline of say 24 or 48 hours. Your two experiences must be no further apart than this.

♦ To count as a coincidence the events involved must not have an obvious causal connection. For example, it would not count if you read the same thing in two books that were about similar subjects.

♦ The dream part of the coincidence must come before the waking life part.

♦ A dream coincidence must link up with either a waking experience or with somebody else's dream. The same thing happening in two of your own dreams does not count.

You may find that when you begin to record coincidences they begin to appear a lot more frequently in your life. Why does this tend to happen? Is it simply because we are tuned into them and noticing them? Or is it because we somehow encourage them to happen by paying attention to them? If you experience dream coincidences, study the related symbols and events carefully. Look out for key words, puns and prominent characters. Ask yourself:

♦ What could this coincidence mean?
♦ Why is this message appearing in different ways in my life?
♦ If a person or animal figures in the coincidence, try to decide if it could reflect an aspect of you.
♦ Does your coincidence prove to be a meaningful synchronicity or is it just a random coincidence? Both types of coincidence are interesting to record and study.
♦ Can you explain your coincidence? If so, it is not really a true coincidence. Remember that the events in a coincidence must be apparently unrelated in what has caused them.

EXPLORING OTHER TYPES OF DREAMS

We have already had a look at some of the more common dream themes in Chapter 7. Here is a further selection of dream types that you may come across.

Dreaming lucidly

A **lucid dream** is one where you become aware that you are dreaming. With practice it is possible to do this on purpose and then take control and make events go the way you want them to, as Sarah did with her monster. A good way to begin exploring this skill is by incubating dreams – you can read more about this in the next chapter.

Forecasting the future

Precognitive dreams – those where we seem to predict future events – may take the form of a warning or coincidence, or both. The incident involved may be of great importance, but more often they seem to be curiously random and trivial.

I once dreamed that somebody handed me a coin with a man's head on it, and some foreign writing that looked like Greek. Next day I went to the bank, and the lady in front of me in the queue handed a coin to the cashier. She explained that she had been given the coin in some change, but it was a foreign one. The lady did not know where the coin was from, but the cashier looked at it and said that it was a Greek coin.

This is a typical precognitive dream: it felt deeply meaningful and interesting, but it didn't give me any major insights or warnings – it simply seemed to show a kind of time-warp in action. Nobody really knows why or how such dreams occur, but many people who keep dream journals soon find that they crop up regularly. Like coincidences, they seem to occur more often when you begin to show an interest in them. In fact, you could argue that all coincidence dreams are also precognitive to some extent. I enjoy precognitive dreams because they suggest that the universe is a lot stranger and more intertwined than we tend to think it is!

Past life dreams

People often dream about characters, events and places from the past – this is quite natural. You might dream that you are back at school, or in a house that you lived in as a child. But what if the dream doesn't seem to relate to your own life in any way? Some people believe that such dreams may be related to past lives, especially when they are part of a series of recurring dreams. It's a fascinating idea, even if you don't believe in reincarnation. What inspires you about this period of history? What aspects do you dislike? How does it make you feel generally? How do you feel about the character that is 'you' in the dream? You might be inspired to learn more about the period of history you have dreamed about and perhaps verify some of the things that you saw.

Dreaming of death

This can be a very frightening dream, where you dream of your own death, or that of a loved one or a well-known person. It can occasionally come as a health warning or as a precognitive dream. More often, however, the death involved is not a physical death. It is more of a psychological death, to do with the death of old belief systems or ways of behaving. Therefore the death dream can be very empowering, bringing a feeling of much-needed release.

It is important to remember that death can be seen as the beginning of a new life, as well as the ending of the old. It is often a case of 'out with the old, in with the new'. The change that is coming into your life may feel difficult and frightening, but it is most likely ultimately for your own good. We tend to resist change through fear of the unknown and clinging on to the familiar. If you dream of death, ask yourself:

♦ What feared change could my dream represent?
♦ Is there an aspect of my life that I know needs to change?
♦ Are you about to embark on a new job, a move, a new relationship or other major change?
♦ Are you worried about your health, or that of a friend or loved one?

Wish-fulfilment dreams

Earlier we discussed the fact that one of the functions of dreaming can be wish-fulfilment. The type of dream where your secret desires come true can be fun and liberating, but on the other hand it tends to leave you with a vague feeling of disappointment when you wake.

If you find that you are often experiencing this type of dream, then it is fairly obvious that your waking life is not as fulfilling as you would like it to be. Try to pinpoint the areas of life that are not satisfying to you, and then set about finding ways of improving the situation. For example, supposing you have a recurring dream about being king of a vast empire. This would suggest that in waking life the opposite is true and you often feel insignificant and powerless. There could be many ways of improving this feeling – perhaps a change of job would help or even a new creative hobby. Try to get in touch with your real needs.

Sexual dreams

Sexual dreams are a natural part of the dream world and tend to appear regularly. Studies have shown that creative people tend to have more of them – possibly because freedom of expression generally is linked with freedom of expression sexually. The important thing is not to feel guilty about your sexual dreams, even if you find yourself enjoying a good time with somebody who is totally unavailable in real life! Remember that the sexual urge is a normal aspect of living in a physical body.

Surprisingly, it is quite common to dream about having sex with somebody that you don't fancy at all in waking life. People also sometimes find that they have rather surprising sexual dreams involving animals and so on. In this case it is important to remember that each aspect of your dream can be thought of as reflecting an aspect of you. So if you dream you are making love to a horse, for example, then think about what aspects of 'horse' you feel are energising and exciting. Remember that the dreaming mind is not restricted by moral censorship. When you have a sexual dream, consider:

♦ Who are you with?
♦ Is this person an appropriate real-life partner or not?
♦ Do you actually fancy this person in waking life?
♦ What is the setting of the dream? Is it a safe private place, or is it somewhere public or dangerous in some way? If you feel exposed, you are probably experiencing some anxiety at the moment.
♦ If you are in a house, consider what messages the house gives – for example, a Victorian setting might suggest repression. Places like hotels and airports suggest a transitory, impersonal feeling.
♦ If you have an unusual sexual dream, such as making love with an animal, or (if you are usually heterosexual) with someone of the same sex, then take note of how you feel. Do you feel disgusted and embarrassed, or is the dream exciting and liberating? Remember, these dreams may link up with your creative and energetic urges.
♦ Is your sex dream a wish-fulfilment dream?

QUESTIONS AND ANSWERS

What if I have a recurring dream that I cannot fathom out?
Try discussing it with a friend. This often opens up your ideas. Alternatively, just before dropping off to sleep, try asking yourself for another dream that will clarify the problem. When you wake up, write down all the dreams you can remember, even fragments, and see if you can connect any of them with the original dream. The connections may not be apparent straight away.

What if I feel that my sexual dream is 'odd' or disturbing?
There are therapists who are trained to help if you really feel that you have a problem. Don't be afraid to seek help and reassurance.

Supposing I have a warning dream involving another person? Should I tell them about it or not?
This is a tricky one. It partly depends on how well you know the person – you don't want to get labelled as a complete crank! You should also consider whether the person is someone who is easily upset. If so, it could be counter-productive to get them into a nervous state, which might, after all, prove totally unnecessary. On the other hand, if you know the person well and you feel that the warning could be relevant, perhaps you might tell them about your dream. Stress that it was just a dream, and leave it up to them to decide whether or not to take action.

CHECKLIST

♦ Do you believe that it is possible to foresee future events in a dream? Do you have any personal experience of this?
♦ How do you think warning dreams arise? Do you think they come from within ourselves, or could external forces be at work too?
♦ If you suffer from nightmares, don't ignore them – try to find out their cause and work with them.
♦ You may find it interesting to begin a record of coincidences that occur in your dreams.
♦ What are your views on reincarnation and past lives? Have you had any dreams that might relate to a past life?

- ◆ Take heed of any personal warning dreams you have – they usually occur for positive reasons.
- ◆ If you dream of death, don't be too frightened. Remember the dream may symbolise your fears about an important change in your life. Take note of any possible health warnings too.

Expanding your dreams 9

LEARNING SIMPLE VISUALISATION TECHNIQUES

You can work with your dreams in greater depth if you learn how to do simple visualisation techniques. We have already begun look at these earlier in the book when, for example, you wrote about your dream house. During this exercise you were encouraged to be inventive and write down all your ideas, even if they did not actually seem to be a part of your dream. A creative visualisation is very like a dream, only you do it when you are actually awake.

Getting properly relaxed

It is important to be well relaxed before trying out a visualisation exercise. You may have your own favourite method of getting relaxed. Have another look at the ideas in Chapter 2. If you find it hard to get properly relaxed, try the following routine:

♦ Find a comfortable position, either sitting or lying down.
♦ For the next few minutes, just concentrate on your breathing. Don't try to alter it at all, simply observe the process. If your attention wanders, keep bringing it gently back to your breathing. After a while your breathing will probably begin to slow down as you start to relax.
♦ Now, starting with your toes, and working slowly upwards, scan each part of your body for tension. If you find tense muscles, take a deep breath in and really tighten them up. Hold the tension for a few seconds. Then on the out-breath, consciously release the tension and let go. Visualise all the tension leaving your body and soaking away into the ground.

♦ You should now feel much more relaxed and ready to begin your visualisation.

Exploring a garden

The following visualisation is a good one to try first. You need to get a friend to read it to you while you relax, or you may prefer to read it aloud yourself onto a tape before you start. Make sure that you don't rush the reading, and leave spaces whenever you see dots like this . . . When you are more used to doing visualisations you may find it possible just to read them through beforehand and then go straight into them without needing to use the spoken words. You can change this visualisation, using plants that are more familiar to you if you wish.

The visualisation

You are standing at the gate of a walled garden. Have a good look at the wall and then study the gate . . . When you feel ready, open the gate and go inside the garden. All around you are beautiful flowers and trees. Stand still for a moment and enjoy the rich colours and scents of the garden . . . Now you notice a little pathway going further into the garden, so you begin to walk slowly along it. There are lavender bushes on either side of the path, and fat bees are buzzing peacefully among the purple blossom. Listen to their summer sound, and smell the wonderful scent from the lavender . . .

After a while you come to a bed of roses. What colour are they? You bend down and cup one of them in your hand and inhale deeply of its scent. Linger for a little while to enjoy the rose bed . . . Now you walk on and you come to a fruit tree laden with one of your favourite fruits. Why not pick one of the fruits and enjoy its taste . . .

When you are ready, walk on again until you come to a little seat in the sunshine, partly shaded by a tree. Sit here for a while and relax in your garden. What do you see? Perhaps there are birds among the leaves of the tree. Fluffy white clouds sail across a blue sky . . . What do you hear? A bird sings in the branches above your head and the leaves rustle in the breeze . . . What do you feel? The sun is warm on your skin and you feel the cooling breeze . . .

You are now free to explore your garden for as long as you wish. It is your own secret place and you can return here whenever you want to. When you are ready, follow the path back to the gate. Don't forget to close the gate when you come back out of your garden.

Being creative with visualisation

You may find it rather difficult to manage visualisations at first. Some people are naturally good at it and already use visualisations in their daydreams. Others do not tend to think in such a visual way. If you are one of these people, try visualising a familiar scene first. Imagine that you are standing in your own living room, for example. Look around you and notice as much as you can. Then gradually go on to visualise slightly less familiar surroundings, such as your local supermarket. Then try inventing a location – try imagining yourself on a tropical island, or at a funfair. After that, try being on the seashore or deep in a forest. The possibilities are endless – just be creative and have fun.

Creative visualisation represents an interesting state of mind that seems to be halfway between dreaming and being fully conscious. The mind is given free rein and allowed to be wonderfully creative, and yet we remain conscious and in control.

RE-ENTERING YOUR DREAM

Once you become good at creative visualisation, you can use the technique to re-enter a dream. In other words, you can replay a dream sequence by visualisation, and then carry on with or alter the dream if you wish, or bring it to a satisfactory ending. This is especially useful for certain types of dreams.

Confronting fear

You can re-enter a nightmare and confront your fear. During a visualisation, you can be much more in control of the situation, so you can change the dream until it no longer disturbs you.

Working on recurring dreams

If you have a persistent recurring dream, you can go back into the dream and try to find out what it is really about. Ask yourself, 'Why am I here again?', 'What is this dream telling me?' You may find that you get a new angle on the dream. Perhaps a new character appears, or the story takes a slightly different course. Remember that you are in control and can make the visualisation progress in whichever way feels best.

Reworking a dream

If you have had a dream that you feel has an unsatisfactory outcome, you can re-enter the dream in order to finish it in a way that feels satisfying. For example, supposing you dream that you look into a mirror and find yourself looking haggard and unwell. You could re-enter this dream and change it by seeing your face radiant and healthy. This would help to remove the negative self-image that has been suggested by the dream. You might even imagine yourself with a new hairstyle and some clothes that really look good on you.

Re-entering a dream gives you a chance to introduce new characters or change existing ones. You can also change the storyline or alter the script in any way you wish. It is rather like being your own film director and it can be both fun and illuminating. It is a good idea to record the dream re-entry in your dream journal in the same way as you would record an ordinary dream.

JO DREAMS THAT LUCY FALLS DOWN A TOWER

Jo dreams that she is in a castle tower with her small daughter Lucy. Lucy is swinging about above the stairs. Suddenly she loses her grip and falls. Jo knows that she has fallen to her death and feels an agonising sense of loss. When she records the dream, Jo feels very upset and frightened by it. But when she thinks it through she realises that she recently felt she had 'lost' Lucy when she started school. The dream also reflects the old fear she had felt when she started school herself.

Jo decides to re-enter this dream and change things. She visualises Lucy just before she falls, swinging from the ceiling of the tower.

Jo asks Lucy why she is doing this. Lucy says, 'I'm showing you how clever I am. I'm a big girl now.' Jo understands that Lucy is beginning to want a little bit of independence. She decides to spread a safety net under Lucy, rather than stop her climbing. When Lucy falls again she falls safely into this net. She thinks this is great fun and bounces about happily in it. Jo feels happy too, because the child is now safe.

INCUBATING DREAMS

Once you are really used to catching your dreams and recording them, you can begin to try incubating dreams. This means deliberately asking for a dream that will help you with a specific problem. For example:

♦ Why am I finding it difficult to stick to my diet?
♦ What can I do to improve my relationship with my sister?
♦ Why do I feel so tired at the moment?

Incubating a dream is related to creative visualisation, because we are actually thinking about our dream before we go to sleep. In effect we are 'ordering' a particular type of dream or selecting certain contents, so it's a bit like setting your TV programmes to be recorded in advance. We have already looked at examples of this – for example in Chapter 4, when I showed you how to encourage certain colours to appear in your dream.

As you are settling down for sleep and getting comfortable in bed, simply focus on your question or problem and say to yourself, 'I would like a dream to help me with . . .'. You don't have to say this out loud – inside your head is fine, or even better, write it down in your dream journal. This helps your unconscious to focus on the question while you sleep. You can also ask for a dream to clarify the meaning of a previous dream. For example:

♦ What did my dream about the white horse mean?
♦ Why do I keep on dreaming about keys?

Asking for help

Dream incubation is particularly helpful if you want advice on a particular problem. For example, you might want to ask questions about your health, or a troublesome relationship. Or you might want to order a dream to help clarify a previous dream. You can use your dream stone to help you with this (see Chapter 2), or you might want to choose an appropriate picture to place by your bed. Oracle decks such as the Tarot are very useful for this. Another good method is to write about your problem in your journal just before you drop off to sleep and ask for a dream to help you. You might also want to ask for help from your dream guide.

ASKING FOR INSTANT SYMBOLS

Asking yourself for an instant symbol is like doing a mini-visualisation. The method can be used for help with any type of problem, as well as for gaining more insight into a dream message. The message is simple – you just ask your question and then close your eyes and ask for a symbol that will help you to arrive at an answer. The trick is to catch the first symbol that pops into your mind, even if it seems an odd choice at first. The symbol must arise totally spontaneously, before your conscious brain has a chance to step in, so catch that first image, however fleeting it is. Try to describe this symbol to yourself, or to a friend. Go into as much detail as possible.

SARAH ASKS FOR AN INSTANT SYMBOL

Sarah feels that she is putting on weight and yet she feels unable to stick to a diet, so she wonders what to do about it. She asks herself for an instant symbol. The symbol that arrives first is a spade. Sarah describes her symbol like this: 'I can see a spade. It is for digging in the earth. I am outside in the garden digging. I need more fresh air and exercise. The spade is for digging deeper.'

She decides that this means she should 'dig deeper' into her own psyche, so she asks for a second instant symbol. This time she sees a clear, sparkling waterfall. Sarah remembers having read that

*one ought to drink plenty of water in order to avoid retaining
fluid. She begins to drink more water and to her surprise she loses
several pounds straight away.*

This example shows how one can work with instant symbols in
order to gain insight into problems from the waking world. You can
work on obscure dreams in the same way. Simply ask for a symbol
that will give you further insight into what your dream is trying to
say. Remember that the process of describing your instant symbol is
very important. You can use the instant symbol method to help with
many of life's choices and problems, such as:

♦ Why am I stuck in this situation again?
♦ What is the best path for me to take?
♦ What is blocking my progress?
♦ How is this person affecting me?

PROTECTING YOURSELF IN YOUR DREAM

Using the creative visualisation method, it is possible to create
special weapons or guardians that you can call upon in the dream
state. Sometimes we wake up in the middle of a nightmare in a
state of fear. If this happens to you, it can be helpful to grasp your
weapon or call upon your guardian before drifting back to sleep
again. You may even find that they appear spontaneously in a dream
once you are used to them. The type of weapon or guardian you
choose is entirely up to you – whatever makes you feel safe is right
for you.

Choosing a protector or weapon

Your dream protector or weapon will be something that makes you
feel safe and empowered. You might already know what it is – if not,
you can use the instant symbol method to find out. Simply relax and
then close your eyes and ask to be shown the best way of protecting
yourself in dreams. You can use your protector or weapon for
defence, warding off enemies and healing. It could be one of the
following, or you may wish to explore your own ideas:

- ◆ *A special crystal* – you may already have a crystal that you can imagine taking with you into the dream world. If not, you can invent one.
- ◆ *A weapon* such as a sword, a laser gun or a small dagger.
- ◆ *An amulet* – this can be any small symbolic object that you can wear about your body. People have made themselves amulets for many thousands of years, often dedicating them for protective purposes with special magical powers. Sometimes amulets are animal or human form, in which case you may find that they 'come alive' and work as a guardian as well.
- ◆ *A special light* – this might be a lantern, or even just a candle. It will illuminate your dark places and make you feel safe. This can be very helpful if you were afraid of the dark as a child. In fact, many adults are still secretly afraid of the dark too – so if you are one of them, don't forget to create a dream lantern.
- ◆ You might also like to imagine a special **suit of armour** that you can put on to protect yourself. An alternative is a protective bubble, or a force field that you can generate at will.

Meeting your guardian

The guardian is a dream figure who will protect and guide you. You can choose any form of guardian that appeals to you. If you do not already have a guardian, try doing a visualisation exercise and ask to be taken to a place where you will meet your guardian. You could start off in the dream garden, or anywhere that feels right to you. The guardian can take any number of forms:

- ◆ The **angel** is a common form of guardian. People feel that angels have great spiritual powers and have a much wider view of things than humans.
- ◆ **Animal** guardians may be very varied. Perhaps you will choose a fierce, strong lion or a swift, far-seeing hawk.
- ◆ Your guardian may be a **human being**, such as a knight in shining armour or a wise old hermit.
- ◆ There are many **mythical beings** that make good guardians too. You could choose a mysterious unicorn or a fire-breathing dragon, for example.

Your guardian may talk to you about problems that arise in your dream work. He or she may also give you gifts, or special powers that will help you during your dream journeying. A guardian may also guide you to your correct path in life, or introduce you to a special task that you must accomplish.

Once you have met your guardian, he or she may appear from time to time in your dreams. You can also ask your guardian to help you with a dream re-entry session. If you feel tense or upset before you go to sleep, ask your guardian for help and don't forget about any special protector or weapon that you can use as well.

FINDING YOUR PLACE OF PEACE

Once you become familiar with the method of creative visualisation, you can try choosing a special place of peace that you can visit at any time. This can be any place that makes you feel peaceful and safe. It could be a wonderful garden, a place by the sea, a crystal cave or a wood full of beautiful trees. It is entirely up to you – just use your imagination and create a place that is right for you.

Begin by relaxing and concentrating on your breathing. Then close your eyes and ask to be taken to your special place of peace. Imagine that you are walking along and you come to a flight of steps. There are twenty of them in all, going downwards. As you go down them, count from one to twenty slowly. You will then find yourself in your special place. Use all your senses to imagine this place as fully as possible. This is your own private place, where nobody else can go.

When you want to become fully awake again, walk back up the twenty steps, counting from twenty to one. Open your eyes and stretch your body gently until you feel awake.

Using your place of peace

You can visit your place of peace whenever you feel stressed. It is a good idea to go there just before you go to sleep. It is also a good place to meet your guardian when you want help with a problem. You will probably find that you add bits to your place of peace gradually as time goes on and you think of more ideas. The main thing is to enjoy your special place and feel really at home there.

QUESTIONS AND ANSWERS

What if I find an unexpected guest or strange beast in my place of peace?

Ask what brings them there and whether they have a special message for you. Remember that you are in control – this is your place. If necessary, evict them!

I find it difficult to do visualisations because I keep getting distracted by external sounds and unwanted thoughts. What can I do?

Keep practising by doing a little bit each day. If you have a spare five minutes when you are alone, just do a mini-session. You will probably find it gradually gets easier and you will be able to extend your period of concentration.

I find it really hard to visualise things at all, but I would like to use the method to work on dream re-entry. What can I do?

Some people do not think in a very visual way and find the method difficult. You could try writing your dream down as a story and then adding to it and re-telling bits of it until it feels right. Or you could draw or paint your dream.

CHECKLIST

◆ Practise creative visualisation whenever you can, even if it is only for a few minutes at a time.

♦ Learn how to work on your dreams by re-entering them and altering things that are not right for you.

♦ If you have a problem, try using the instant symbol method to help you to arrive at a solution.

♦ Begin to work with protectors and guardians who will help you in the dream world.

♦ Find your place of peace and visit it often.

10 *Working with other people*

RUNNING A DREAM GROUP

Starting your group

When you have become more confident with working on your own dreams, you may like to consider working with other people in a small group. If you are unable to find a suitable group in your area, you could consider joining a group online or starting your own group. Many of the sections in this chapter are equally good for solo exploration – for example, the sections about art and creative writing.

You could begin by sharing your dreams with other members of your own family. This can help partners and children to express their feelings more openly. If this idea does not seem right, perhaps you have a few good friends who would be interested in starting up a dream group. You could consider advertising your group, but bear in mind that this means you may be working with total strangers.

A dream group might form naturally as you begin to discuss your dreams with other people and gradually discover that you have a mutual interest. There are quite a few advantages of working together on your dreams, instead of working alone all the time:

- Sharing a dream can make the dream more significant.
- People in the group can offer one another mutual support and acceptance.

♦ You can gain new insights into your dreams when you do group work. These come partly from feedback from the other members of the group, and partly from the impact of speaking your dream aloud.

♦ It is fun sharing dreams and relating within the group.

Your dream group doesn't need to be formal in its approach. In fact, you may like to combine the dream work with other shared activities, such as having a meal together. Each member could bring his or her own contribution of food or drink. This works well – nobody has all the work to do and it gives the occasion a feeling of enjoyable fun and sociability. Each person needs to bring his or her dream journal along as well.

Discussing what you want from your group
When you decide to set up your dream group, there are a few points to consider at the first meeting:

♦ Begin by letting each person talk about themselves for a few minutes as a form of introduction. You don't need to go into great detail, just let the others know who you are and what your main interests are.

♦ Decide where you are going to hold your meetings. Usually a private house is the best place, and you may find that it is best to rotate houses, going to a different one each time. This means that the job of hosting the event is shared.

♦ How often do you want to meet? About once a fortnight is probably ideal, but this may not suit all members.

♦ Decide on the number of members you want. A small group of no more than half a dozen or so is best. This means that all the people get a chance to talk about their dreams, and members don't feel inhibited by revealing their innermost thoughts to a whole lot of people.

♦ Clarify the aims of the group by discussing what each person hopes to get out of meeting. This helps to get to know one another better.

♦ You might like to discuss having a small ceremony at the beginning of each meeting. This could be as simple as lighting a candle and sitting in silence for five minutes before you begin. A ceremony like this helps to set the atmosphere and calm everybody down a bit before you begin to share your dreams.

The idea of working in a group is not to interpret other people's dreams for them. If you do that, as often as not you are just projecting your own ideas onto them, and may be barking up the wrong tree. Try instead to ask questions and offer suggestions. If a person feels that your suggestion is not right, allow them to reject it. Similarly, don't feel that you necessarily have to take other people's ideas about your own dreams on board.

SARAH FORMS A NEW DREAM EXPLORERS GROUP
Sarah mentions her interest in dreams to four friends and between them they decide to form a dream explorers group. They agree to meet every other Wednesday at one another's houses. Meanwhile, Sarah explains to her friends how to keep a dream journal. The group decides that it would be fun to share a meal before going on to do their dream work. The hostess of the week provides the main course and the others bring drinks, salad, pudding and chocolate! Everyone soon feels that they are gaining a lot of mutual support, and look forward to their evenings together.

JAMES JOINS AN ONLINE DREAM WORK GROUP
When James describes an interesting dream of his to a friend at work, it turns out that she is also interested in dreams. She suggests that he try joining her online dream explorers group. James is uncertain at first about sharing his dreams publicly, but he decides to give it a try. He discovers that the people in the group are friendly and supportive, and soon begins to get fresh insights into his dreams. Once he gets to know the other people better, he feels more able to open up and discuss many of his dreams.

ACTING OUT YOUR DREAM

Using the whole group

The dream group setting gives you an opportunity to work with your dream further by acting it out. This can help to bring a dream to life and see how characters can interact. Two or three members of the group are chosen to act the main characters. Usually the person whose dream it is takes the lead role. He or she can also be the director, or sometimes another person can be chosen to do this.

To begin, read out the dream and then allow any comments to arise as to how the dream should be acted out. When the dream 'play' is underway, try to allow the characters free rein. The idea is not really to act out a strict version of the dream, so much as to allow the characters to develop in any way that seems appropriate. Acting out a dream is more like a dream re-entry.

◆ You can alter the storyline or the script as you go along.
◆ A different ending can be allowed to emerge if it seems helpful to the dreamer.
◆ The characters can feel free to express whatever emotions they wish. This is especially valuable for dreams involving fear or anger.
◆ Other group members can supply support and encouragement. For example, they could supply a cushion to beat up if a person expresses rage, or stand by to comfort people who get upset.

Acting out dreams in this way can be very valuable because people feel supported by the rest of the group and feel that their emotions are being validated.

Acting your dream solo

Another variation on acting out your dream is where the dreamer chooses to act out all the roles. This works best with dreams where there are only two main characters. A chair or cushion is placed to represent the position of the two characters. The dreamer then acts out the two characters in turn, physically moving position whenever the other character speaks.

Fig 11   A dragon – monster or guardian?

This method is very good for dreams where you want to get a new angle on the viewpoint of a character in your dream. For example, supposing you are being pursued by a monster in your dream. Try asking the monster why it is pursuing you. Then swap chairs or cushions, and actually be the monster. Allow the monster to have its say, then swap back into your own role, and so on.

EXPANDING DREAM DIALOGUES

During sessions of acting out a dream you will probably find that interesting dialogues develop between the characters. The dialogue need not necessarily have occurred at all in the original dream. You can take this a step further and imagine that you actually meet a dream character and then hold a conversation with that character. This can be useful for developing dreams that feel especially important or revelatory to the dreamer. It is also good for working with nightmares, such as Sarah's Tall Flobbery Monster dream. Dialogues develop best when the dream group members know one another well and feel safe within the group setting.

Developing a dialogue

If a character keeps persistently turning up in your dreams, it can be a good idea to develop a dialogue of this sort. The dreamer becomes the character, and other members of the group pose questions to him or her. Sometimes it is not clear why a character is appearing in your dreams until you actually become that character. Then the words seem to take over and the character comes alive. Remember that you can see each character in your dream as an aspect of yourself, or as an aspect of an important relationship or problem in your life.

With a little practice you can become very imaginative and hold conversations not only with human characters, but also with animals and even inanimate objects from a dream. For example, Jo keeps dreaming about a table, so she decides to hold a conversation with it, talking to Sue, another member of her dream group.

Sue: Who are you?

Jo: I am a table.

Sue: Why do you keep appearing in Jo's dreams?

Jo: Because I'm in Jo's house.

Sue: Where are you in the house?

Jo: In the kitchen.

Sue: What are you for?

Jo: The family sit around me to eat and talk about stuff.

Jo realises that the table is an important focal point for the family. She finds that as she begins to discuss some of her dreams with the children, they become interested too and dreams soon become a regular topic of conversation at the breakfast table. Jo finds that this helps her to understand when something is bothering one of the children. She gets interested in the subject of children's dreams and does a little research on the internet. Then she begins to wonder if she could do a course on child development, maybe through the Open University.

GETTING CREATIVE WITH ARTWORK

Drawing or painting your dream is an excellent way of exploring it in more depth and this can be an exciting group activity. Each person can choose a dream, not necessarily their own, that they would like to work with. You can either try to depict a whole scene from the dream, or else you can chose one particular aspect, such as a symbol, a colour, an animal, a monster and so on. You don't need to be a great artist, so don't worry about the way the picture looks. The point is to try to express ideas in a new way. Your group might also like to try out some of the following ideas:

- Make a picture of a nightmare, or a horrifying image from a dream.
- Try illustrating a recurring dream. Which aspects emerge as being the most important ones in the picture?
- Try to recall a childhood dream and then draw a picture of it.

♦ Use a large sheet of paper and divide it in half. On one half illustrate an unhappy dream. On the other half of the paper, try to draw the same dream but this time with a happy ending.

♦ Each person in the group closes their eyes, asks for an instant symbol, and then does a picture of their symbol. Can you find any connections between the images produced by your group?

♦ Draw a detailed picture of a dream house or a house that you visualise in your mind.

♦ Get the whole group to relax and visualise a special place of peace. Then either create individual pictures or work on a large group picture which incorporates everyone's ideas.

♦ Create pictures of your inner child when he or she is happy, sad and angry.

♦ Try illustrating a favourite fairy story or myth. You could just choose one special aspect of the story if you wish, such as a dragon or a magical sword.

♦ Make a **mandala**. This is a personal power symbol, usually round in shape. Choose symbols and colours from your dreams that have empowered you. You can add to your mandala gradually, building it up until it really means something to you personally.

WRITING FROM YOUR DREAMS

This is another idea for exploring dreams that works well in a group setting. You can write a story based on one of your own dreams, or you can use someone else's idea. Your group may like to try some of the following, and then explore further ideas of your own:

♦ Write a story based on your worst nightmare. Add to it and embellish it as you wish.

♦ Describe a nasty dream monster in as much detail as you can.

♦ Write about meeting your inner child. Describe the setting where you meet as well.

♦ Choose an interesting dream character and write a short story involving that character.

♦ Write a detailed description of a dream house. What alterations and home improvements would you like to make?

♦ Think about means of transport that you have come across in dreams and write about some of them. Which ones appeal to you most and why?

As with acting and drawing your dream, you don't need to be restricted by sticking to the original dream. Use the dream as a starting point and allow your imagination to run riot.

Story-telling

Another variation on creative writing is to have a story-telling session. One person starts the ball rolling with an idea from a dream, and then the next person takes up the theme and carries on with the story. This can carry on for as long as you wish and it can get quite hilarious.

QUESTIONS AND ANSWERS

What if someone in my dream group is causing friction with others?

This is a frequent problem in a group setting. In the long run the best thing to do, although it is often not easy, is to discuss the problem openly and honestly. You may find that your group will shed members after a while! Bear in mind that groups are rarely static and people may leave once they have gained all that they can gain from being in the group.

What if I feel too embarrassed to discuss a dream?

Then don't. There is no rule that says you have to. You may find it easier later on, when you get to know and trust the other members.

What if someone insists that my dream means something that doesn't resonate with me?

Tell them how you feel. Point out, gently but firmly, that this is your dream and only you are the expert on your own dreams.

CHECKLIST

♦ If you decide that you would like to join a dream group, check your local paper or library to see if you can find one. If not, why not consider starting your own locally, or join one online?

♦ Make the sessions in your dream work group enjoyable and relaxing. Never force your interpretations on another person. Get the group to consider:
  – The most valuable aspects of working in a group.
  – To what extent group members' dreams reflect their different personalities.
  – New ideas for group activities.

♦ When the group has become well established, write down 'anonymously' the outline of dreams you might find it hard to talk about openly. Pool the pieces of paper, get each person to pick one out at random and discuss common areas of difficulty. Maintain respect for each others' anonymity.

♦ Remember to keep your dream journal and dream dictionary up to date.

♦ Have fun!

A *short dream dictionary*

This is a very short dream dictionary to start you off. The interpretations are not cast in stone – your ideas may well be different.

Accident. A message that you need to slow down and take more care of yourself.

Aeroplane. Looking at things from a higher viewpoint. Going up in the world.

Angel. This may be a special dream messenger, so listen carefully. Angels represent higher, spiritual ideas. Your angel may be a guardian angel who takes care of you.

Animal. Take note of the type of animal and listen to your instinctive feelings. (See Chapter 6.)

Attic. The highest part of the house may represent your spiritual self. Also look and see what is *in* your attic. You may find things which you have stored away from the past and now need to be looked at again.

Baby. A new beginning, idea or insight. Is your baby contented or are you neglecting it or refusing responsibility for it? It may also represent your own 'inner baby' – the part of you that longs to be pampered and totally secure.

Baggage. Stuff that you are lugging about that you probably don't need any more. Resentments.

Basement. The hidden part of the psyche where you store stuff that you are afraid of. The root of a problem.

Bed. Security and warmth. Escaping from the real world. Sexual issues.

Bell. Can be a joyful omen or a warning. Look at the context in your dream.

Bird. Take note of the type of bird and listen to your instinctive feelings. (See Chapter 6.)

Blood. Life force. Anger and fear. Menstrual blood represents feminine power, fertility and release.

Boat. Water in dreams usually represents our emotions and the boat shows how we are coping with them. Is it a peaceful journey, or are you sailing on rough, frightening water?

Book. A lesson is being offered to you. What is the book about?

Bottle. You may be bottling something up. What does your bottle have in it? Is the lid on or off? What colour is the bottle?

Cage. Feeling trapped. Fear – are you making the cage yourself? Are you in it, or does it contain a fierce animal or another person?

Car. A means of moving on. Is the car under your control? It may represent your physical self.

Cards. Fate – what sort of hand you are being dealt. Divining the future.

Cave. The hidden, unconscious, inner self. A very primitive, archetypal dream symbol. Initiation. Sanctuary.

Child. Your own child, or a child you know? Or an inner child self? The dream may be about something that brings back feelings from childhood, such as fear, helplessness or uninhibited joy.

Church, or other religious building. Authority. Religious ideas. Faith, security, sanctuary. Depends a lot on your own views on religion.

Climbing. Working upwards towards a goal. Is it hard work or easy going? If you are climbing downwards you are probably beginning to explore your unconscious mind.

Clothes. The persona – the self that you present to the outside world. If the clothes are outlandish, you may want to express yourself more. If too tight, you are growing out of your present image. Or maybe you just need to go on a diet!

Crying. Expressing emotions that you are not letting go of in your waking world. You need to pay attention to what this dream is saying.

Crystal. Clarity and purity. Also depends on the type of crystal or stone. (See Chapter 2.)

Dancing. Feeling happy and uninhibited. Abundant energy.

Dawn. A new beginning. Something is dawning on you.

Death. A complete change. Releasing and letting go of the past. May also be a warning about your health or that of another. Who is dying in your dream? What energies or type of situation does that person represent to you?

Devil. Fear. Temptation. Somebody who manipulates you. Lust and earthly passions. May represent a part of you that you see as 'bad'.

Door. A way through. A transition. If it is open, you are ready for new discoveries.

Earthquake. An upheaval, especially an emotional one. Fear of changes that you see approaching.

Explosion. Sudden personal crisis. Often to do with a relationship.

Falling. Loss of control. Falling down on the job. Letting go. Partly depends if you are simply falling over, or falling into something or down something.

Fire. A dangerous situation, especially an emotional one. Sexual energy. Spiritual energy. Enthusiasm. Dramatic new beginning.

Flood. Overwhelming emotions. Release.

Flowers. Messages of happiness and grace. Spiritual guides.

Flying. Astral travelling. Rising above your everyday world onto a more spiritual level. Freedom. Initiation.

Fog. Uncertainty and confusion. Concealment.

Food. Can represent any kind of nourishment: physical, emotional, spiritual. Depends also on the kind of food, for example sweets for the sweet things in life, sausages may be phallic, etc. Are you enjoying the food?

Garden. Your place of peace. Doing something creative. Look at the plants in your garden: is it full of lovely flowers, or are there lots of weeds to be sorted out?

Gate. A way through, perhaps to another world, or to a new phase of your life. New opportunity.

Hair. Often comes into dreams if you are concerned about your physical self, especially if your hair seems to be falling out (quite a common dream). Combing hair – getting rid of tangles in your life. Healthy hair – good health.

Hotel. A transition in your life, a temporary situation. Feeling unsettled.

House. Often represents the self. A large rambling house can mean that you are beginning to explore your own psyche. The house can represent your physical or spiritual self – so if there is something wrong with the house, look for connections, for example the roof blowing off could indicate a situation in which you feel very exposed and vulnerable. (See Chapter 5.)

Island. Feeling isolated or self-contained. A place of refuge.

Journey. Personal growth. If your journey is delayed, look at ways in which your progress is being blocked. The means of transport is also important, and so are any people who are travelling with you. (See Chapter 5.)

Judge. Your own alter-ego – that is, the part of you that judges your own actions. Your inner parent. Make sure that you are not being over-critical of yourself.

Key. The way forward, the means of opening a door. This may be on a physical or a spiritual level.

Killing. Something in your life that you need to get rid of. Maybe old behaviour or beliefs that are no longer appropriate. If it is a murder, then the situation probably involves anger. You may find that you are killing an animal. If so, what sort is it? If you are killing a child, this may represent some childish behaviour.

Mine. A hidden source of treasure or strength. Going down deep into the unconscious.

Mirror. The mirror is showing you some aspect of yourself or your behaviour that you need to face.

Money. May show that you are worried about money. Richness of experience. Profitable actions. Energy.

Moon. A powerful symbol of feminine psychic energy. Tides and rhythms, going with the flow, menstruation. New moon – new beginnings. Full moon – power and completion, fertility. Waning moon – getting rid of unwanted emotions.

Music. A beautiful dream symbol which may mean getting in touch with powerful spiritual forces. If the music is not harmonious, however, you are out of tune with something.

Nest. Safety and cosiness. Family and home. Incubating ideas.

Net. Trying to catch something – an idea perhaps? Or perhaps you feel trapped, unable to escape.

Path. Your life's path, the way to go. Look to see if the way is easy, or is it uphill or overgrown?

Policeman. An authority figure. Guilt. What are you doing that you see as bad? Alternatively it may be a sign of care and protection.

Postman. Messages coming into your life. What sort of news does he bring?

Race. The rat race. Are you trying too hard to compete? Winning a race may represent a personal victory of some sort.

Rainbow. A symbol of faith and joy. A promise of better times ahead. Often appears after a period of emotional problems.

Ring. Marriage, promises, completion, love.

Rock. Safe place, strength. Or alternatively, being dashed against the rocks. An obstacle of some sort.

Roof. Feeling of security and safety. The roof is the top of the house, so it may show you the condition of your spiritual self.

Running. Depends partly if you are running *away* from something that you fear, or running *towards* something exciting. If you are running away, try to stop and face the truth. Running fast may indicate acceleration in your spiritual growth.

School. Lessons to be learned, or a situation that reminds you of your childhood.

Seasons. *Spring* – New beginnings. *Summer* – Fertility, growth, strength. *Autumn* – Harvesting, letting go. *Winter* – Resting, waiting, end of a cycle.

Stairs. *Going up* – success, rise in confidence, going up to more spiritual levels. *Going down* – Loss of confidence, or exploring the unconscious.

Star. Hope and guidance. Something to look forward to. Higher beings who are showing you the way.

Sun. Joy and success. Confidence. Strength. Situation improving after a difficult time.

Sword. Attack or defence. Finding the truth of a situation.

Teeth. Often shows concern about your physical body. Wanting to attack or bite somebody. *Teeth falling out* – physical illness, or a transition time, such as that you went through as a child, when your teeth *really* fell out.

Telephone. Messages and communication. Are you answering it?

Toilets. Getting rid of stuff you no longer need. May also be connected with deep-seated guilt or anxiety. Preparing to do something/go somewhere.

Trees. What kind of tree? Personal development. Spiritual guidance. Family matters. Is your tree small or large, straight or crooked? Has it got leaves on at the moment?

Uniform. Authority. Conforming. Are you being too rigid in some way? Or do you feel this about somebody else?

War. Anxiety and anger that is inside you and liable to erupt. Conflict.

Washing. Cleansing something, letting go.

Water. Emotional matters. Look at the type of water, where it is, what condition it is in, how deep it is and so on. (See Chapter 5.) Fluid thinking.

Waterfall. Emotional release. Healing.

Web. Connectedness. Alternatively, feeling trapped or caught. Are you weaving it yourself? A complex situation.

Wheel. Life's ups and downs. Luck, good fortune. Travel.

Window. Looking at a situation in a different way. Looking at the future or the past. Seeking alternatives.

Glossary

Affirmation. An empowering statement used to encourage a positive state of mind.

Archetype. A universally recognisable image, or pattern of thinking, which represents a typical human experience.

Astral body. Ethereal counterpart of the body; supposed to travel far afield in dreams and to survive after death.

Coincidence. Events or circumstances that appear to be connected, but not in a causal way (that is, one does not follow on from or cause the other). A synchronicity is a coincidence that seems meaningful in some way.

Collective unconscious. The deepest layer of the unconscious, which extends beyond the individual psyche. It is concerned with ancestral memories and experiences common to all mankind.

Dream-catcher. A decorative net hung above the bed to encourage dream recall, and disperse nightmares.

Essential oil. Volatile oil derived from a plant and used in aromatherapy.

Free association. A method of exploring spontaneous ideas arising from a given word or symbol.

Imagery. Pictures seen with the mind's eye.

Inner child. The part of the psyche that is still child-like and holds memories from childhood.

Lucid dream. A dream during which one becomes aware that one is dreaming.

Mandala. Symbolic circular figure that represents the universe, or the self's search for wholeness.

Myth. A traditional story that tries to explain natural, social or religious phenomena.

Precognition. Knowing beforehand, often by apparently supernatural means.

Projection. A defensive process whereby an unconscious characteristic, a fault or even a talent of one's own is seen as belonging to another person or object.

Psyche. The whole of a person's inner, mental world. The mind, soul or spirit.

Shadow. The unconscious part of the personality that contains characteristics one cannot recognise as one's own.

Symbol. A thing that represents, typifies or recalls another thing.

Unconscious. Parts of the mind and personality we are not aware of, but that still influence our thoughts and actions.

Visualisation. The experiencing of visual imagery.

Further reading

Dream blog by Ruth Snowden, with lots of further ideas and discussions: www.exploringdreams.blogspot.com

Books by Ruth Snowden
Understanding Freud, Hodder, ISBN 978-1444-12255-8
Understanding Jung, Hodder, ISBN 978-1444-12245-9
Freud – the key ideas, Hodder, ISBN 978-1-444-10328-1
Jung – the key ideas, Hodder, ISBN 978-1-444-10329-8

Other books
The Interpretation of Dreams, Sigmund Freud (many editions available)
Man and His Symbols, Carl Jung (many editions available)
The Dream Dictionary From A to Z, Theresa Cheung, 2009
Lucid Dreaming, Stephen Laberge, 2009
The Aromatherapy Bible, Gill Farrer-Halls, 2009

Cygnus Books
www.cygnus-books.co.uk
A huge selection of books and CDs on health, personal growth, spirituality and environmental issues. Cygnus Books also produces a monthly review, which makes interesting reading and will keep you up to date.

Kindred Spirit
www.kindredspirit.co.uk
A bi-monthly magazine devoted to positive change, which has articles on spiritual growth, personal development, complementary therapies, travel, health and much more.

Index

Some other titles from How To Books

CHALLENGING DEPRESSION AND DESPAIR
A medication-free, self-help programme that will change your life

ANGELA PATMORE

This book is offered as a lifeline to people at the bottom of the bottomless pit of depression.

It will explain the research and the thinking behind the 'tough love' approach, much of which may be new to you because it flies in the face of current trends. With positive, common sense strategies, this book enables you to regain emotional control, showing that it is possible to combat depression without resorting to drugs or costly and often ineffective therapy.

The first part of the book offers fresh insights into depression and into how it can be overcome. The second offers practical advice culminating in a series of challenges that will enable you to change your entire attitude to emotional health and achieve a more positive and hopeful outlook on life.

ISBN 978-1-84528-439-8

88 CHINESE MEDICINE SECRETS
How to cultivate lifelong health, wisdom and happiness

ANGELA HICKS

In China, people send greetings by wishing a person 'a long and healthy life'. Our natural state is to be healthy and happy. This includes having a calm mind, a healthy body and emotional resourcefulness.

This book reveals the profound, yet simple health maintenance secrets that Chinese medicine has developed over many centuries. These secrets enable you to deal with stress and return to your natural balance. By practising these secrets you will learn how to recover the ability to nourish and protect your energy, overcome illness and feel an easy joy in simply being alive.

Angela Hicks has been a practitioner of Chinese Medicine for over 30 years and is joint principal of the College of Integrated Chinese Medicine in Reading, UK.

ISBN 978-1-84528-430-5

DON'T SHOOT – I'M NOT WELL!
Confidence for when you really need it

SEÁN BRICKELL

This book contains some powerful, practical, confidence techniques that will transform your work and life with immediate effect.

- Do you want more social confidence to make you more popular?
- Do you want more emotional confidence to make you more attractive?
- Do you want more confidence at work so you get paid more and promoted?
- Do you want the confidence to enjoy more adventure and excitement in your life?
- Do you want the confidence to grab more life-changing opportunities?

If the answer to any of these is 'Yes', then the highly practical and realistic *Don't Shoot – I'm Not Well!* will give you the skills and the mindset you need. The techniques in the book will help you deal with rude, bitchy and patronising people; ask women or men out; gain sexual confidence; deal with a critical partner or parent; network effectively; cope with setbacks; and more.

ISBN 978-1-84528-457-2

DIY SEX AND RELATIONSHIP THERAPY

DR LORI BOUL WITH DR JUNE KERR

Consulting a sex and relationship therapist is very expensive, yet much of the work in sex and relationship therapy is done by the couple on their own. Although therapists and counsellors are trained to help people in a variety of ways, their role is mainly to provide education by acting as facilitators or mediators: their clients are the 'real' experts on their relationship. A lot of the work done by therapists is directed at giving couples 'homework' exercises to be carried out before the next session. This means that couples are largely responsible for their own success. This book can help you to overcome your problems yourselves without paying out huge fees to therapists. It will teach you skills that can make your intimate relationships more satisfying and assist you in rekindling the fun and romance.

ISBN 978-1-84528-474-9

HEALING FOODS, HEALTHY FOOD
Using superfoods to help fight disease and maintain a healthy body

GLORIA HALIM

Cutting out processed and junk foods from your diet and introducing the superfoods listed in this book can help you to boost your immune system and increase your energy levels. Superfoods are rich in vitamins, minerals and anti-oxidants. This book lists them individually and explains why they are so good for you and how they can help keep you healthy. It also lists a number of spices which have medicinal benefits in their own right. By combining these spices with some of the superfoods, this book includes some simple but delicious recipes that have their roots in the Mediterranean, Asian and African regions, all of which are known for having the healthiest diets in the world.

ISBN 978-1-905862-53-5

FIBROMYALGIA AND MYOFASCIAL PAIN SYNDROME

A practical guide to getting on with your life

DR CHRIS JENNER

There really is life after being diagnosed with fibromyalgia or myofascial pain syndrome . . . and yours starts here. The lack of knowledge which surrounds two of the most prevalent illnesses in the world today means that they can often go undiagnosed and untreated for years, during which time both the mental and physical condition of sufferers can deteriorate considerably.

With the right care, there is much that can be done to help anyone with these conditions to improve their quality of life dramatically. The first step towards that is by doing precisely what you are doing now, educating yourself.

Within the covers of this book, you will find an easy-to-read and practical guide to dealing with fibromyalgia and myofascial pain. Dr Chris Jenner takes a straightforward and down-to-earth look at what these two conditions are about; how they might affect different aspects of your life; what your options are; and how you can get on with your life.

Dr Chris Jenner has studied for many years in the field of Pain Medicine and works with sufferers of these and other chronic pain conditions in his roles as consultant in Pain Medicine and Anaesthesia at St Mary's Hospital, London, and as Director of London Pain Consultants.

ISBN 978-1-84528-467-1

NECK AND BACK PAIN
A practical guide to getting on with your life

DR CHRIS JENNER

Far from just being the curse of the elderly, neck and back pain affects the majority of the adult population at some point in their lives, as well as huge numbers of children and adolescents. Even in chronic cases, however, it does not have to mean the end of life as you once knew it. With the knowledge contained in this book and the right care, you *can* regain control and live a happy and productive life. In his reassuringly down-to-earth guide, Dr Chris Jenner describes the many causes of neck and back pain in easily understood laymen's terms. He then explores what it means to live with neck and back conditions in a practical sense, sets out your treatment options, and advises on how you can very greatly reduce your levels of pain and increase your quality of life.

Dr Chris Jenner has studied for many years in the field of Pain Medicine and works with sufferers of these and other chronic pain conditions in his roles as consultant in Pain Medicine and Anaesthesia at St Mary's Hospital, London, and as Director of London Pain Consultants.

ISBN 978-1-84528-468-8

How To Books are available through all good bookshops, or you can order direct from us through Grantham Book Services.

Tel: +44 (0)1476 541080
Fax: +44 (0)1476 541061
Email: *orders@gbs.tbs-ltd.co.uk*

Or via our website
www.howtobooks.co.uk

To order via any of these methods please quote the title(s) of the book(s) and your credit card number together with its expiry date.

For further information about our books and catalogue, please contact:

How To Books
Spring Hill House
Spring Hill Road
Begbroke, Oxford OX5 1RX

Visit our web site at
www.howtobooks.co.uk

Or you can contact us by email at *info@howtobooks.co.uk*